Edexcel GCSE History (9–1)

Superpower relations and the Cold War 1941–91

Kat O'Connor
Tim Williams

SERIES EDITOR
Aaron Wilkes

OXFORD
UNIVERSITY PRESS

Great Clarendon Street, Oxford, OX2 6DP, United Kingdom

Oxford University Press is a department of the University of Oxford.
It furthers the University's objective of excellence in research, scholarship,
and education by publishing worldwide. Oxford is a registered trade mark
of Oxford University Press in the UK and in certain other countries

© Oxford University Press 2022

The moral rights of the authors have been asserted

First published in 2022

All rights reserved. No part of this publication may be reproduced, stored
in a retrieval system, or transmitted, in any form or by any means, without
the prior permission in writing of Oxford University Press, or as expressly
permitted by law, by licence or under terms agreed with the appropriate
reprographics rights organization. Enquiries concerning reproduction
outside the scope of the above should be sent to the Rights Department,
Oxford University Press, at the address above.

You must not circulate this work in any other form and you must impose
this same condition on any acquirer

British Library Cataloguing in Publication Data
Data available

978-1-382-02985-8

978-1-382-02983-4 (ebook)
978-1-382-02984-1 (Kerboodle)

10 9 8 7 6 5 4 3 2

Paper used in the production of this book is a natural, recyclable product
made from wood grown in sustainable forests.

The manufacturing process conforms to the environmental regulations of
the country of origin.

Printed in Great Britain by Ashford Colour Press Ltd.

In order to ensure that this resource offers high-quality support for
the associated Pearson qualification, it has been through a review
process by the awarding body. This process confirms that this resource
fully covers the teaching and learning content of the specification
or part of a specification at which it is aimed. It also confirms that it
demonstrates an appropriate balance between the development of
subject skills, knowledge and understanding, in addition to preparation
for assessment.

Endorsement does not cover any guidance on assessment activities
or processes (e.g. practice questions or advice on how to answer
assessment questions) included in the resource, nor does it prescribe
any particular approach to the teaching or delivery of a related course.

While the publishers have made every attempt to ensure that advice on
the qualification and its assessment is accurate, the official specification
and associated assessment guidance materials are the only authoritative
source of information and should always be referred to for definitive
guidance.

Pearson examiners have not contributed to any sections in this resource
relevant to examination papers for which they have responsibility.

Examiners will not use endorsed resources as a source of material for
any assessment set by Pearson.

Endorsement of a resource does not mean that the resource is required
to achieve this Pearson qualification, nor does it mean that it is the
only suitable material available to support the qualification, and any
resource lists produced by the awarding body shall include this and other
appropriate resources.

The publisher would like to thank the following people for their help
preparing this book for publication: Sarah Hartsmith and David Rawlings,
and James Helling for the index.

From Kat O'Connor: I would like to thank my husband, my parents and
my colleagues at George Abbot School for their support, patience and
encouragement. My share of this book is dedicated to my wonderful young
son Joe, a historian in the making!

From Tim Williams: Thank you to everyone at OUP for your guidance and
patience, and thank you for once again putting your trust in me. Thanks
also to my incredibly supportive family. I would like to dedicate this book
to the amazing and inspiring colleagues and students who I love working
with every day.

Contents

Introduction to the series 4
Timeline 6

Part 1: The origins of the Cold War 1941–58

Chapter 1: Early tensions between the East and West
1.1 What was the Cold War? 8
1.2A/B Capitalism vs communism 10
1.3 How much of an alliance was the Grand Alliance? 14
1.4 Yalta: the successful conference? 16
1.5 Potsdam: the bad-tempered conference? 18
1.6 What was the impact of the atomic bomb? 20
1.7 The Iron Curtain descends 22

Chapter 2: The development of the Cold War
2.1 Containing communism: what was the Truman Doctrine? 24
2.2 What was the Marshall Plan? 26
2.3 How did the USSR respond to the Marshall Plan? 28
2.4 Berlin divided 30
2.5 The Berlin Crisis: Stalin's blockade 32
2.6 The Berlin Crisis: the airlift and its impact 34

Chapter 3: The Cold War intensifies
3.1 The arms race 36
3.2 NATO and the Warsaw Pact: new alliances 38
3.3 How real was 'the thaw' after Stalin's death? 40
3.4 'Seven days of freedom': the Hungarian Uprising, 1956 42
3.5 How did Khrushchev and the world react to the Hungarian Uprising? 44

Exam practice 'Explain two consequences…' questions 46

Part 2: Cold War crises 1958–70

Chapter 4: Flashpoint: Berlin
4.1 Berlin: Khrushchev's ultimatum and the 1961 Vienna Summit 48
4.2 'Close the border!' The Berlin Wall 50
4.3 'Ich bin ein Berliner': the USA's reaction to the Berlin Wall 52

Chapter 5: Flashpoint: Cuba
5.1 America's backyard: revolution in Cuba 54
5.2 What happened at the Bay of Pigs? 56
5.3A/B The Cuban Missile Crisis 58
5.4 The consequences of the Cuban Missile Crisis 62

Chapter 6: Flashpoint: Czechoslovakia
6.1A/B The Prague Spring 64
6.2 How did the world respond to the Prague Spring? 68
6.3 What was the Brezhnev Doctrine? 70

Exam practice 'Write a narrative account…' questions 72

Part 3: The End of the Cold War 1970–91

Chapter 7: Changing relationship between the superpowers
7.1 The start of détente: hope for better relations 74
7.2 A false dawn: the reality of détente 76
7.3 The Soviet invasion of Afghanistan, 1979 78
7.4 The USA's response to the Soviet invasion of Afghanistan 80
7.5 What was the Second Cold War? 82

Chapter 8: The collapse of the Soviet Union
8.1A/B Gorbachev's 'new thinking' and the Sinatra Doctrine 84
8.2A/B How did the Soviet Union lose its grip on Eastern Europe? 88
8.3 The fall of the Berlin Wall 92
8.4A/B The collapse of the Soviet Union and the end of the Cold War 94
8.5 Why did the Cold War end? 98

Exam practice 'Explain two of the following' questions 100

Glossary 102
Index 106
Acknowledgements 110

Introduction to the Edexcel GCSE History series

Oxford's *Edexcel GCSE History* series has been specially written by an expert team of Edexcel teachers and historians. Each chapter matches the content of the Edexcel specification. Written in an engaging style, the eye-catching pages are organised into clear sections with a logical route through the historical content.

Extensive use has been made of photographs, diagrams and maps; there is a lively mix of visual and textual **Sources** and **Interpretations** to captivate and challenge you. We have worked really hard to uncover some hidden gems that will add so much to your understanding of the topics.

The **Work** activities and **Exam-style questions** have been written to help you check your understanding of the content and develop your skills as a historian. The activities are designed to suit all abilities, and will properly prepare you for your GCSE exams.

You can develop your knowledge and understanding further at home and in class through the interactive activities, animations, film clips with historians, On Your Marks exam questions, revision quizzes and more on Kerboodle.

Superpower relations and the Cold War

This textbook guides you through one of Edexcel's Period studies: **Superpower relations and the Cold War 1941–91**. Period studies focus on a time span of at least 50 years and require you to understand how a substantial issue or development unfolded during that time. You will study the causes and events of the Cold War: how and why conflict occurred, and why it proved so difficult to resolve the tensions that arose. You will need to understand the whole story, from early tension between East and West in the 1940s, through to the collapse of Soviet control of Eastern Europe and the end of the Cold War in the early 1990s.

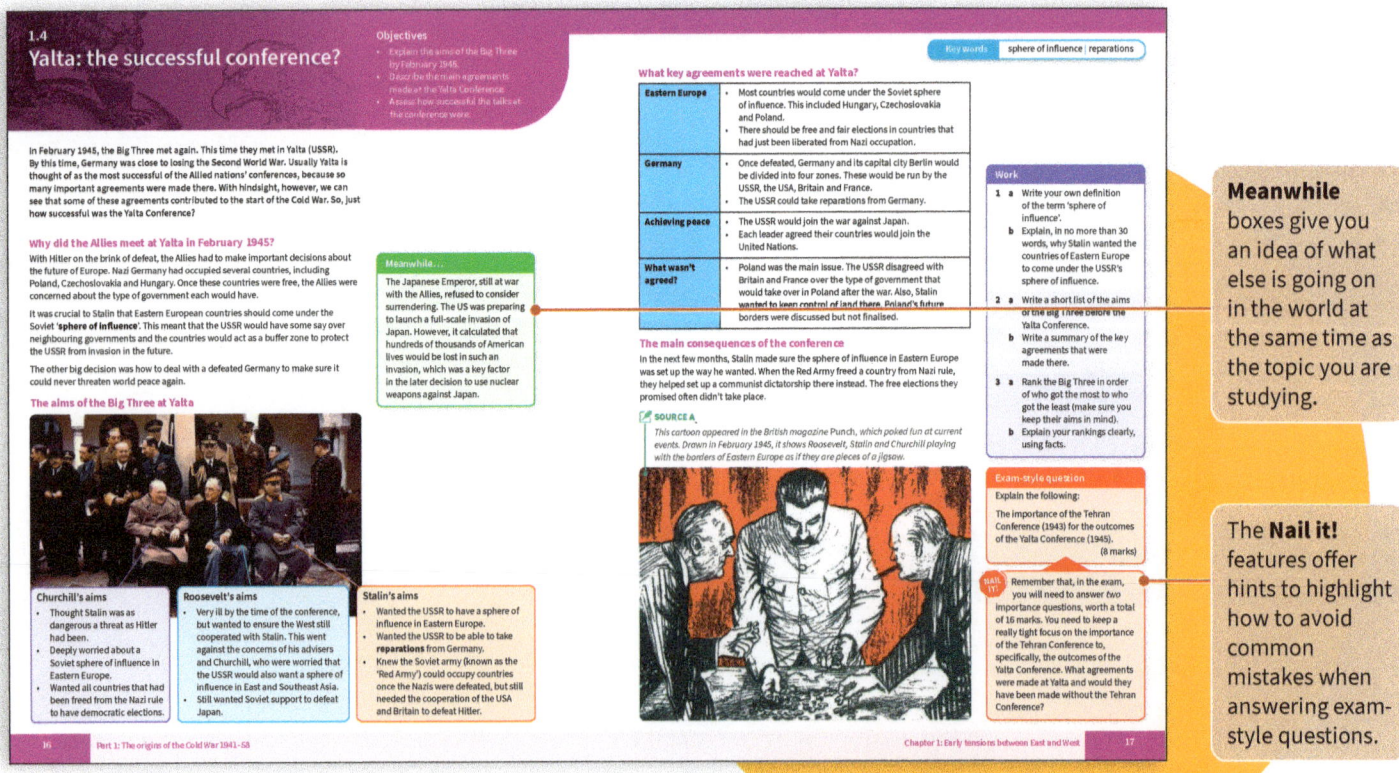

Meanwhile boxes give you an idea of what else is going on in the world at the same time as the topic you are studying.

The **Nail it!** features offer hints to highlight how to avoid common mistakes when answering exam-style questions.

How to use this textbook

Written for the Edexcel specification, the features in this textbook include:

Objectives
- Learning objectives at the beginning of each lesson are based on the requirements of the Edexcel course – so you can be confident you are studying what you need to know.

Key words
Important phrases and terms are highlighted. Learn what they mean – and how to spell and use them correctly.

SOURCE / INTERPRETATION
Sources introduce you to evidence that is primary or contemporary to the period, and **Interpretations** provide you with different people's perspectives on the past.

Work
1 The activities and questions aim to develop your knowledge, understanding and key history skills. They are designed to be progressive in terms of difficulty, and to get you to become familiar with the history and apply what you have learned.

Meanwhile
This gives you an idea of what else is going on in the world (perhaps in another country) at the same time as the period you are studying in the lesson.

Exam-style question
These questions help you practise your exam skills. They give you an idea of the types of questions you might get in an exam.

NAIL IT! These are hints to highlight key parts of Exam-style questions and will help you answer them.

Earlier on / Later on…
This feature gets you to make connections between the topic you are studying and events, ideas or developments that happened many years before or many years in the future.

Timeline
A short list of dates identifying key events to help you understand chronology.

1956

Exam practice
These pages are designed to help you apply what you learn to the Edexcel GCSE History exam. They take you on a step-by-step journey to help you write clear, focused answers to each of the GCSE question types you will encounter in your exam.

Introduction 5

Timeline
Superpower relations and the Cold War 1941–91

This textbook covers the period of the Cold War, beginning during the Second World War and lasting until the early 1990s. It focuses on relations between the two superpowers – the USA and the USSR – and examines the causes, events and consequences of the most significant moments of their rivalry. It considers how and why conflict occurred, and why disagreements were often so difficult to resolve. The timeline on these pages highlights some of the key events of the period.

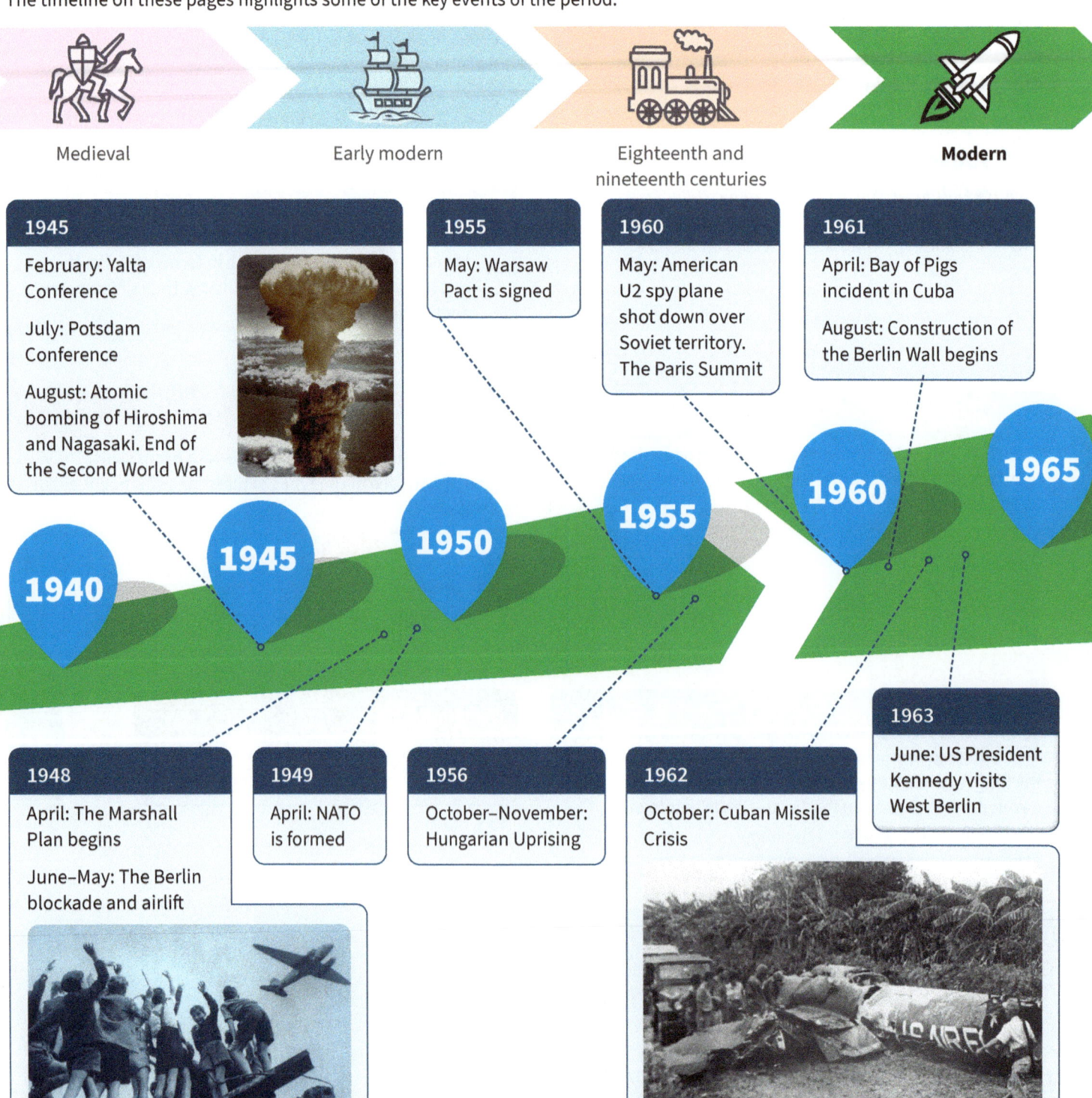

Medieval | Early modern | Eighteenth and nineteenth centuries | **Modern**

1945
- February: Yalta Conference
- July: Potsdam Conference
- August: Atomic bombing of Hiroshima and Nagasaki. End of the Second World War

1955
- May: Warsaw Pact is signed

1960
- May: American U2 spy plane shot down over Soviet territory. The Paris Summit

1961
- April: Bay of Pigs incident in Cuba
- August: Construction of the Berlin Wall begins

1940 — 1945 — 1950 — 1955 — 1960 — 1965

1948
- April: The Marshall Plan begins
- June–May: The Berlin blockade and airlift

1949
- April: NATO is formed

1956
- October–November: Hungarian Uprising

1962
- October: Cuban Missile Crisis

1963
- June: US President Kennedy visits West Berlin

6 Superpower relations and the Cold War 1941–91

1989

Eastern European independence movements, including the fall of the Berlin Wall in November

1991

December: Collapse of the USSR

1968

January–August: Prague Spring

1970 **1975** **1980** **1985** **1990** **1995**

1972

May: SALT I signed

1979

December: Soviet troops invade Afghanistan

1981

January: Reagan becomes US president

1985

March: Gorbachev becomes leader of the USSR and introduces his 'new thinking'

1.1 What was the Cold War?

Objectives
- Define the terms 'superpower' and 'Cold War'.
- Describe the two sides and the reasons for their difficult relationship.
- Explain how the Cold War developed.

The relationship between two powerful countries – the USSR and the USA – was the most important global issue of the second half of the twentieth century. When relations were bad, the world held its breath, fearful of war on a scale that had never been seen before. Despite these fears, there was never actually any direct fighting between the two countries. What took place was the Cold War, a period of tension and mistrust that nearly brought about global destruction on several occasions. What caused the Cold War? How did it develop over time? What was its impact on the world?

The two superpowers

The Second World War (1939–45) caused huge destruction and suffering. Countries with very different political systems had worked together to defeat their common enemies. The USA and the USSR had been **allies**, fighting together against Nazi Germany, but once victory had been achieved the two sides began to lose trust in each other.

The USSR and the USA both emerged from the Second World War as **superpowers** – countries that were much more powerful than any others because of their strong military forces and large **economies**. As no fighting had taken place on mainland USA during the war, its economy was still strong because farmland, factories and transport systems had not been damaged. In contrast, the USSR had suffered greatly because so much fighting had taken place there. However, it gained influence over a number of countries in Eastern Europe and still had a huge military force.

> **Meanwhile...**
> The Cold War was going on at the same time as decolonisation, when a number of countries around the world were gaining independence from empires run by Britain, France, Portugal and others. The USA and the USSR both took a very strong interest in the new governments of these countries, especially in Africa in the 1960s. Both superpowers tried to bring more countries into their own sphere of influence. They used various methods to do this, including military and economic methods.

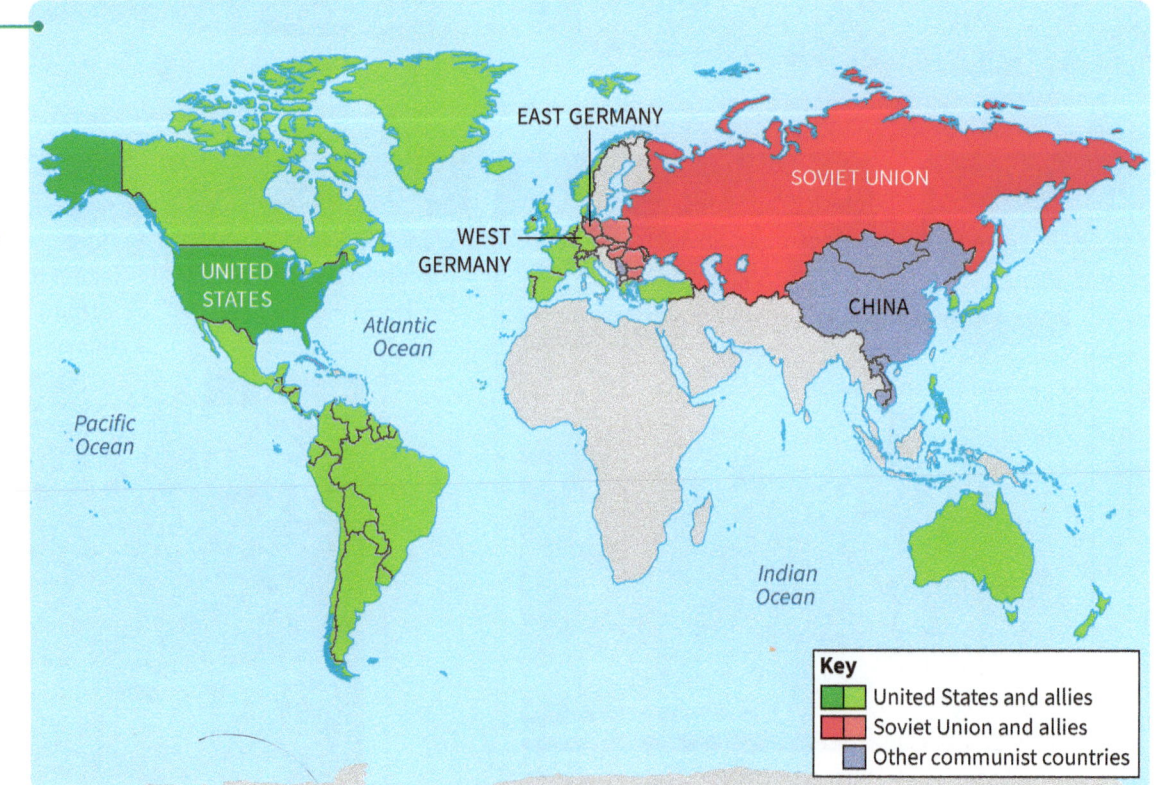

A

The areas of the world that were either controlled or influenced by the two superpowers during the **Cold War**. Some countries were able to make this choice freely, others were not. The USA and the countries influenced by it are often grouped together and referred to as 'the West', and the USSR and the countries influenced by it are often grouped together and referred to as 'the East'.

8 Part 1: The origins of the Cold War 1941–58

| Key words | allies \| superpower \| economy \| Cold War \| nuclear weapon \| Mutually Assured Destruction (MAD) \| propaganda \| proxy war |

Who exactly were the two sides?

The United States of America (USA): a capitalist democracy (see pages 10–11) in North America. Sometimes referred to as America or the United States.

The Union of Soviet Socialist Republics (USSR): a collection of countries controlled by Russia from 1922 to 1991. It was governed under the communist system (see pages 10–11). Sometimes referred to as the Soviet Union.

Earlier on …

The word 'Soviet' referred to the councils that were set up by workers to run Russian towns at the start of the twentieth century. From the 1920s, it became a general term to describe the people, government and military of the Soviet Union.

B

The Socialist Republics that made up the USSR

The Cold War

From the end of the Second World War onwards, the two superpowers were locked in a strong rivalry with each other. At times the tension between them was so high it looked as if war might actually break out. At other times they worked together to try to end the areas of conflict between them.

Early on, both sides were the first countries in the world to develop **nuclear weapons** (the USA in 1945 and the USSR in 1949) and these increased in number and strength throughout the period. These weapons made the consequences of war much greater than ever before and led to the idea of **Mutually Assured Destruction (MAD)** – both sides knew that the use of nuclear weapons could destroy the world and wipe out all civilisation! The superpowers were therefore keen to avoid direct military conflict. Instead, the rivalry was played out through spies, secret missions and **propaganda**. It was also fought through **proxy wars** in which each side would supply weapons to other groups fighting against each other. Proxy wars of the Cold War era include the Korean War (1950–53), the Vietnam War (1955–75), and the Soviet–Afghan War (1979–89).

SOURCE C

A cartoon published in the American newspaper the LA Times in 1945, drawn by Bruce Russell. It is common for the USSR to be represented by a bear and the USA to be represented by an eagle. The text on the pieces of paper reads 'irresponsible statements' and 'deepening suspicions'.

Work

1. Explain the terms 'Cold War' and 'superpower' in your own words.

2. Why were the USA and the USSR able to emerge from the Second World War as superpowers, when other countries were not?

3. Look at **Source C**.
   a. What point is this source making about the situation in 1945?
   b. How far does this reflect the situation at the time?

Chapter 1: Early tensions between East and West 9

1.2A Capitalism vs communism

Objectives
- Describe capitalism and communism.
- Compare key features of the USA and the USSR.
- Explain why the very different ideas behind capitalism and communism meant the superpowers saw each other as a threat.

After the end of the Second World War there were two very different sets of ideas about how people should live and be governed. These two ideas – capitalism and communism – were so opposed to each other that the USA (which was capitalist) and the USSR (which was communist) felt threatened just by the other's existence. So what were these vastly different ideas? How did they affect the relationship between the USA and the USSR? And why were these countries referred to as 'superpowers'?

Where did these two ideologies come from?

The sets of ideas about how people should live and be governed are known as ideologies. They affect all parts of life in a country. The USA and the USSR – the world's largest superpowers – had very different ideologies.

Capitalism

This term mostly describes how an economy works. Under **capitalism**, businesses and individuals are free to make as much money as they can. Interference from government (for example, high taxes or rules about workers' rights) is kept to a minimum.

Americans were also strong believers in **democracy**: the idea that people should be involved in choosing who governs them. The USA was (and still is) a capitalist democracy.

Communism

Communists had a very different idea about how money should be made and shared compared to capitalists. Under **communism**, the government controls the economy and politicians decide what and how many goods are made, not individual businesses. In theory, this would ensure wealth is shared more equally and there wouldn't be some people who were extremely rich and others who were extremely poor.

Communism as an idea was developed by the political thinker Karl Marx in the nineteenth century. A few decades later, a communist group called the Bolsheviks seized power in Russia following a popular uprising. In 1917, they set up a communist **dictatorship** under Vladimir Lenin.

Lenin and his supporters believed that communism offered working people (the majority of the Russian population) freedom: freedom from poverty and from being treated badly by their employers. However, communism in Russia took away many other kinds of freedom. Lenin argued that this was necessary to protect communist ideas and to stop them being overthrown by greedy capitalists.

> **Earlier on …**
>
> The word 'democracy' comes from the Greek words 'demos' (people) and 'kratos' (rule). Ancient Athens had one of the first democratic governments, in the sixth century BCE. However, women and enslaved people were not allowed to vote.

INTERPRETATION A

Detail from a 1947 Soviet painting called 'Lenin proclaims Soviet power'. It shows Lenin announcing that the Bolsheviks had taken over the government of Russia in November 1917.

10 Part 1: The origins of the Cold War 1941–58

Key words | capitalism | democracy | communism | dictatorship

 **The USA during the Cold War**   **The USSR during the Cold War**

Economic ideas: How money should be made and earned

Capitalism

 Industry mostly owned by private companies

 Freedom to make as much money as you can

 Often a big difference between rich and poor

Communism

 Industry owned by the state

 Private wealth taken away by the government

 Similar living standards for everyone

Political ideas: How a country should be governed

Democracy

 Free elections

 Freedom of speech

 Individual rights

Dictatorship

 Elections, but only one political party allowed

 Limited individual rights and freedom

 Harsh punishments for criticising the government

Meanwhile…

There were communist parties in Western European countries too, including the Communist Party of Great Britain. During the Great Depression of the 1930s, when unemployment was high, communism appealed to more people, although very few communist parties gained enough votes to win any major elections. Communist parties also lost a lot of members when the brutality of Stalin's regime became widely known around the world.

Work

1. Write a paragraph of no more than 50 words describing one key difference between the USA and the USSR. Do not list features; write full sentences using connectives like 'meanwhile' or 'whereas'.

2. Which groups of people in society do you think would have been most likely to have been unhappy living under communism? Think about who loses out when there is a communist government.

Chapter 1: Early tensions between East and West

1.2B

How was the capitalist USA different from the communist USSR?

The USA

In their daily lives, most Americans had many personal freedoms. **Censorship** was very limited; there was a **free press**. People who could vote had a choice of different political parties and views. There was a consumer boom after the Second World War – this meant there were many new products available and credit schemes making it easier to 'buy now and pay later'. For many Americans, living standards had never been better and the USA prided itself on being a free country.

By the 1950s, the US economy was thriving. The Second World War had devastated many European countries' ability to make food and goods that their people needed, but the USA wasn't affected in the same way because the war wasn't fought on American soil. It could trade goods and resources with war-torn Europe and continue to make money. This is one of the reasons why US governments were so determined to prevent more countries from becoming communist: if they 'fell' to communism, they wouldn't trade with the USA any more because it was a capitalist country.

The USSR

By 1928, Joseph Stalin had made himself leader of the USSR. He ruled as a dictator until his death in 1953. Under Stalin's dictatorship, workers were shown as heroes in propaganda, and before the Second World War people had a reasonable wage and a home. However, there was very little choice: people were generally allocated jobs and housing. Consumer goods were limited. For example, if you wanted a car you put your name on a waiting list and often waited years to get one. The economy provided only a basic standard of living for all.

For many Soviet people, however, the worst part of living under Stalin's version of communism was the political side. Stalin was very paranoid. There were secret police whose job was to listen to people's private conversations and read people's letters. They were looking for signs of disloyalty to Stalin and communism. People suspected of this were often taken from their homes in the middle of the night and never saw their families again. Stalin also used brutal prisons called gulags for political prisoners. There was no legal way of challenging communism or changing the government.

SOURCE A

The front page of an American comic book from 1947. Its purpose was to warn the public of the dangers of potential communist plots to take over the USA.

SOURCE B

A Soviet propaganda poster from 1923. It shows capitalists as greedy and grotesque.

Part 1: The origins of the Cold War 1941–58

Key words: censorship | free press

Tension and suspicion

Before the Second World War, there had already been a great deal of suspicion between the two countries. From the moment the communists seized power in Russia in 1917, the USA saw it as a threat, and vice versa.

Many Western leaders were horrified by the communist takeover in Russia in 1917, and were worried that a revolution might happen in their own countries. Soon after the communists took power in Russia, there was a civil war there. Britain, the USA and other countries sent soldiers to help fight against the communists. The communists won the civil war but never forgot that Western capitalists had tried to crush them. Even though the USA and the USSR were allied during the Second World War, Stalin blamed the West for not stopping Hitler taking over most of Europe earlier. All this was on Stalin's mind at the start of the Cold War.

 INTERPRETATION C

An extract from The Cold War: A New History, *written in 2005 by Lewis Gaddis, a professor of history*

> Thanks to an ingenious constitution, their geographical isolation from potential rivals, and a magnificent endowment of natural resources, the Americans managed to build an extraordinarily powerful state ... They ... severely restricted their government's capacity to control everyday life ... Despite ... persistent racial, sexual and social discrimination, the citizens of the United States could plausibly claim, in 1945, to live in the freest society on the face of the earth.
>
> [In Russia] the Bolshevik Revolution ... had happened only a quarter of a century earlier ... Stalin ... forced a largely agrarian nation [a country whose main industry was farming] with few traditions of liberty to become a heavily industrialised nation with no liberty at all. As a consequence, the USSR was, at the end of World War 2, the most authoritarian [very strictly ruled] society anywhere on the face of the earth.

Work

1. Create a small table with 'USA' as the heading of one column and 'USSR' as the heading of the other. Then put the features below onto the correct side of your table:
   - claimed to support workers' interests instead of big businesses
   - was more democratic
   - had a very paranoid leader
   - believed it had done more to stop Hitler during the Second World War
   - was more economically powerful
   - had a free press that was not censored
   - was a one-party state.

2. In your own words, come up with three slogans (short, memorable phrases) that capitalists might use to make communism sound bad. Then come up with three slogans that communists might use to make capitalism sound bad.

3. Study **Source A**. How could a historian use this image to explain Americans' fear of communism? Use the contextual knowledge you've gained so far.

4. Study **Source B**. How has the artist made capitalism look bad? Try to explain what you can see, such as the spider's web behind the capitalist.

Chapter 1: Early tensions between East and West 13

1.3 How much of an alliance was the Grand Alliance?

Objectives
- Explain the advantages of a USA/USSR alliance during the Second World War.
- Describe the personalities of the 'Big Three'.
- Identify the decisions made by the 'Big Three' in Tehran in 1943.

Before the Second World War there was already deep mistrust between the Soviets in communist USSR and the capitalist countries of the West. However, in 1941 the Soviet, American and British leaders (the 'Big Three') decided to work together in an alliance to defeat Hitler and Nazi Germany. Two years later, in Tehran (Iran), they worked out a plan to do this. What made the Tehran Conference reasonably successful, despite the leaders' differences?

Enemies become allies: the Grand Alliance

At the start of the Second World War, in 1939, the USSR was in an **alliance** with Nazi Germany. That year, both their armies invaded Poland. Germany was also in an alliance with Japan, called the Axis. The USA was neutral when the war started – so it took no sides – but it did send weapons and supplies to countries fighting Germany.

Two surprise attacks took place that shook these alliances:
- In June 1941, Nazi Germany invaded the USSR. This was a deadly military operation costing millions of lives and destroying whole cities. Fighting between Germany and the USSR took place on the Eastern Front between German-occupied areas and the USSR.
- In December 1941, Japan launched a surprise attack on the US naval base at Pearl Harbor, Hawaii. The USA and Japan then fought against each other in the Pacific.

By the end of December 1941, the USSR, the USA and Britain were all willing to join a new alliance – the Grand Alliance – to defeat Germany and Japan.

Meanwhile…

The Grand Alliance was under severe strain at times. For example, in 1943, the graves of 10,000 Polish officers – murdered by Soviet troops – were found in Katyn Forest in western USSR. Churchill and Roosevelt were told of the massacre, but did not address the issue with Stalin because they felt that defeating Hitler was more important than putting the fragile relationship at risk.

A

The Allied and Axis nations during the Second World War at the start of 1942

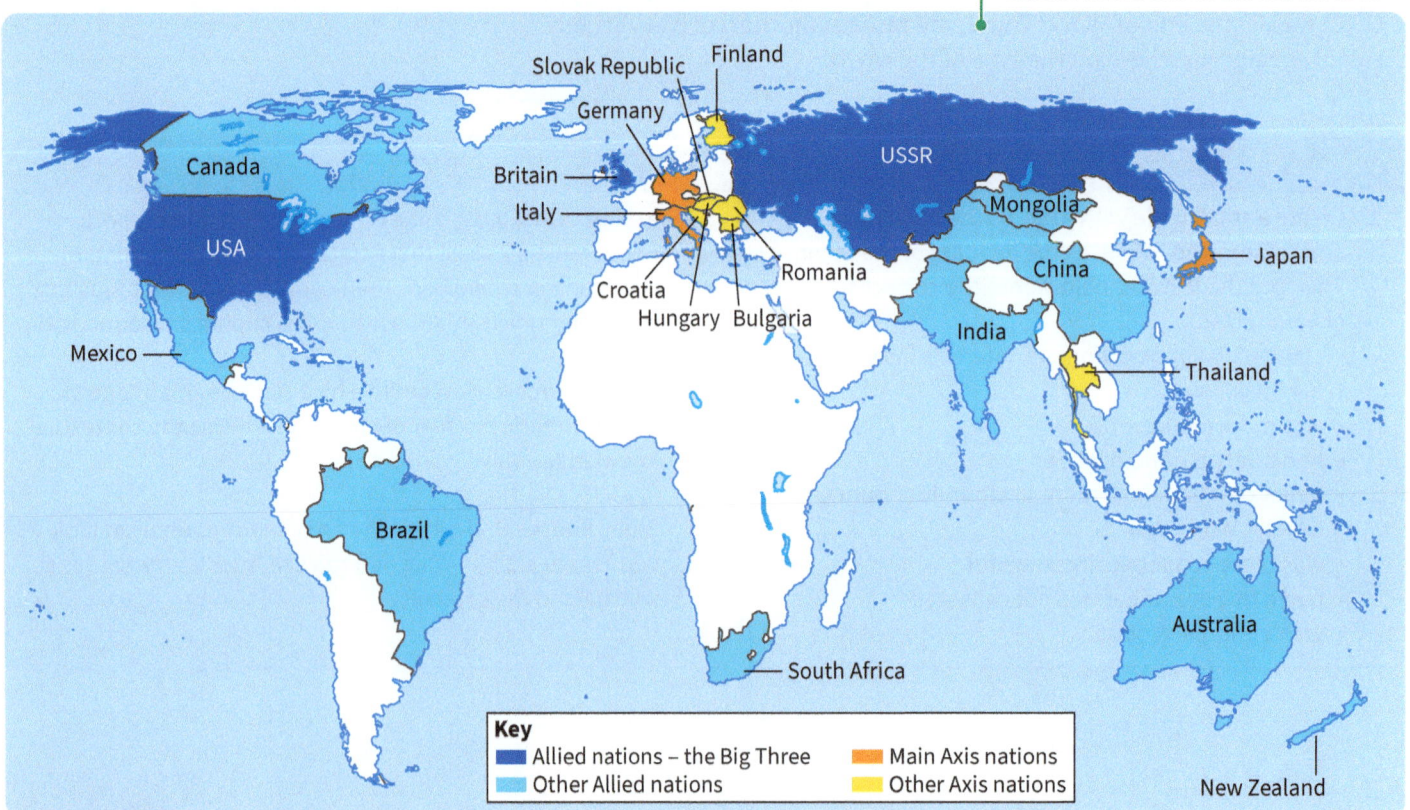

Part 1: The origins of the Cold War 1941–58

Key words   alliance | United Nations

Who were the Big Three?

The leaders of the USA, the USSR and Britain became known as the Big Three because these were the most powerful Allied countries. They met up at conferences and made decisions about the best way to win the war and what would happen to Europe afterwards. To help us understand these decisions, we need to understand the leaders themselves:

Joseph Stalin
- Leader of the USSR
- Ruled as a dictator
- Deeply suspicious of the West despite the Grand Alliance
- Determined that the USSR would not be invaded on its western border

Franklin D. Roosevelt
- Popular US president: he had won elections in 1932, 1936 and 1940, so he could be confident of the support of the American public.
- More willing to work with Stalin than Churchill was: Roosevelt was concerned that the USSR would stop cooperating altogether if some of Stalin's demands weren't met.

Winston Churchill
- British Prime Minister; Churchill had refused to negotiate with Hitler, even in the summer of 1940 when the British had few allies who could help them against Germany.
- Deeply suspicious of Stalin's rule and of communism generally
- Very worried about Stalin's demand for land in Eastern Europe to protect the USSR from future invasion by the West

The Tehran Conference, 1943

When the Big Three sat down together at Tehran (in modern-day Iran) they decided on a plan to invade Nazi-occupied Europe. The invasion began on 6 June 1944 with D-Day.

Stalin agreed that, in the future, the USSR would join the **United Nations**, an international organisation that was set up in 1945 to promote world peace. He and Roosevelt also agreed that the Soviets would join the USA's war against Japan once Hitler was defeated.

Stalin and Churchill, however, had got on less well. Churchill agreed to meet Stalin in Moscow in October 1944 in order to resolve their differences. At this meeting, Churchill and Stalin made the so-called 'percentages agreement'. They agreed that countries in Eastern Europe should be divided between the Soviets and the West when the war was won. Churchill would later regret this.

Work

1. Write a short timeline outlining what the USSR did during the Second World War. Start with: '1939: formed an alliance with Nazi Germany.'
2. How satisfied were each of the Big Three with the agreements at Tehran? Give each leader a score out of 10 for satisfaction. Explain your score.
3. a What signs can you see so far of a Cold War starting to develop between the West and the USSR?
   b Who or what do you think will be the biggest issue making the relationship more difficult later on?

Exam-style question

Write a narrative account analysing the key events that led to the agreements made at the Tehran Conference (1943).

You **may** use the following in your answer:
- the invasion of the USSR by Nazi Germany
- the formation of the Grand Alliance

You **must** also use information of your own.   (8 marks)

NAIL IT! For your first attempt at this question, focus on describing what happened between 1941 and 1943, explaining how one event led to the next. Begin by describing why the USSR became allies with Britain, then why the USA joined the Grand Alliance, then what each leader hoped to achieve at Tehran.

Chapter 1: Early tensions between East and West

1.4
Yalta: the successful conference?

Objectives
- Explain the aims of the Big Three by February 1945.
- Describe the main agreements made at the Yalta Conference.
- Assess how successful the talks at the conference were.

In February 1945, the Big Three met again. This time they met in Yalta (USSR). By this time, Germany was close to losing the Second World War. Usually Yalta is thought of as the most successful of the Allied nations' conferences, because so many important agreements were made there. With hindsight, however, we can see that some of these agreements contributed to the start of the Cold War. So, just how successful was the Yalta Conference?

Why did the Allies meet at Yalta in February 1945?

With Hitler on the brink of defeat, the Allies had to make important decisions about the future of Europe. Nazi Germany had occupied several countries, including Poland, Czechoslovakia and Hungary. Once these countries were free, the Allies were concerned about the type of government each would have.

It was crucial to Stalin that Eastern European countries should come under the Soviet '**sphere of influence**'. This meant that the USSR would have some say over neighbouring governments and the countries would act as a buffer zone to protect the USSR from invasion in the future.

The other big decision was how to deal with a defeated Germany to make sure it could never threaten world peace again.

> **Meanwhile…**
> The Japanese Emperor, still at war with the Allies, refused to consider surrendering. The US was preparing to launch a full-scale invasion of Japan. However, it calculated that hundreds of thousands of American lives would be lost in such an invasion, which was a key factor in the later decision to use nuclear weapons against Japan.

The aims of the Big Three at Yalta

Churchill's aims
- Thought Stalin was as dangerous a threat as Hitler had been.
- Deeply worried about a Soviet sphere of influence in Eastern Europe.
- Wanted all countries that had been freed from the Nazi rule to have democratic elections.

Roosevelt's aims
- Very ill by the time of the conference, but wanted to ensure the West still cooperated with Stalin. This went against the concerns of his advisers and Churchill, who were worried that the USSR would also want a sphere of influence in East and Southeast Asia.
- Still wanted Soviet support to defeat Japan.

Stalin's aims
- Wanted the USSR to have a sphere of influence in Eastern Europe.
- Wanted the USSR to be able to take **reparations** from Germany.
- Knew the Soviet army (known as the 'Red Army') could occupy countries once the Nazis were defeated, but still needed the cooperation of the USA and Britain to defeat Hitler.

Part 1: The origins of the Cold War 1941–58

Key words | sphere of influence | reparations

What key agreements were reached at Yalta?

Eastern Europe	• Most countries would come under the Soviet sphere of influence. This included Hungary, Czechoslovakia and Poland. • There should be free and fair elections in countries that had just been liberated from Nazi occupation.
Germany	• Once defeated, Germany and its capital city Berlin would be divided into four zones. These would be run by the USSR, the USA, Britain and France. • The USSR could take reparations from Germany.
Achieving peace	• The USSR would join the war against Japan. • Each leader agreed their countries would join the United Nations.
What wasn't agreed?	• Poland was the main issue. The USSR disagreed with Britain and France over the type of government that would take over in Poland after the war. Also, Stalin wanted to keep control of land there. Poland's future borders were discussed but not finalised.

The main consequences of the conference

In the next few months, Stalin made sure the sphere of influence in Eastern Europe was set up the way he wanted. When the Red Army freed a country from Nazi rule, they helped set up a communist dictatorship there instead. The free elections they promised often didn't take place.

 SOURCE A

This cartoon appeared in the British magazine Punch, *which poked fun at current events. Drawn in February 1945, it shows Roosevelt, Stalin and Churchill playing with the borders of Eastern Europe as if they are pieces of a jigsaw.*

Work

1. **a** Write your own definition of the term 'sphere of influence'.
   b Explain, in no more than 30 words, why Stalin wanted the countries of Eastern Europe to come under the USSR's sphere of influence.

2. **a** Write a short list of the aims of the Big Three before the Yalta Conference.
   b Write a summary of the key agreements that were made there.

3. **a** Rank the Big Three in order of who got the most to who got the least (make sure you keep their aims in mind).
   b Explain your rankings clearly, using facts.

Exam-style question

Explain the following:

The importance of the Tehran Conference (1943) for the outcomes of the Yalta Conference (1945).

(8 marks)

NAIL IT! Remember that, in the exam, you will need to answer *two* importance questions, worth a total of 16 marks. You need to keep a really tight focus on the importance of the Tehran Conference to, specifically, the outcomes of the Yalta Conference. What agreements were made at Yalta and would they have been made without the Tehran Conference?

Chapter 1: Early tensions between East and West

1.5 Potsdam: the bad-tempered conference?

Objectives
- Describe the situation in Europe by July 1945.
- Explain why the US and Soviet leaders distrusted one another.
- Assess the success of the Potsdam Conference.

In the summer of 1945, another conference took place. The Big Three gathered at Potsdam, just outside Berlin, in July and August 1945. But these were not the same Big Three leaders who had gathered at Yalta in February 1945. Tensions were high. But why? What had changed? Just how bad-tempered was the Potsdam Conference?

What had changed by July 1945?

Soviet occupation

By April 1945, in Western Europe, British and US forces were moving quickly towards Berlin (Germany's capital city). Along the way, they were freeing villages, towns and countries from German occupation. In Eastern Europe, Soviet forces were advancing towards Berlin too. Hitler and his closest followers retreated to an underground bunker beneath Berlin's streets and, on 30 April, Hitler killed himself. Within days, Germany surrendered and the war in Europe was over. However, many people in Eastern Europe were deeply worried about the Soviets occupying their country and setting up communist governments (see page 22 for a map of the USSR's eventual sphere of influence in Eastern Europe). As the Red Army continued to occupy Poland, Hungary, Romania and Bulgaria, the Western leaders became increasingly concerned that the 'free and fair' elections agreed at Yalta would never take place.

A new president

In April 1945, Roosevelt died and his Vice President, Harry Truman, became US president. He was much more anti-communist than Roosevelt. Meanwhile, Churchill lost a general election in the UK and was replaced part way through the Potsdam Conference by the new Labour Prime Minister, Clement Attlee.

A 'powerful new weapon'

The day before the conference, the USA had successfully tested the first ever **atomic bomb**. Truman decided to tell Stalin about this 'powerful new weapon', not mentioning that it was nuclear. The bomb put the USA in a very strong position: it now had a clear military advantage over the USSR. Truman was surprised when Stalin didn't have a strong reaction to the news – but this was because Stalin's spies had already told him about it!

Soviet expansion in Eastern Europe

Once the German army had been defeated and pushed back from countries in Eastern Europe, some Soviet soldiers stayed in these countries. At the Yalta Conference, it had been agreed that the USSR would have a sphere of influence in Eastern Europe, but now Churchill and Truman were worried about how much influence there would be. The Red Army was occupying Poland, for example, and had already helped to set up a communist government there. This went against the agreement of the Big Three to allow countries to hold free, democratic elections.

SOURCE A

Stalin and Truman at Potsdam. The mistrust between the Soviet leader and the new US President was a key reason for the difficulties at the conference.

Part 1: The origins of the Cold War 1941–58

Truman vs Stalin

Truman shared Churchill's concerns about Soviet expansion in Europe. At the conference, it was clear that there was suspicion between Truman and Stalin.

The USA intended to use its new nuclear weapon against Japan. However, this frustrated Stalin because he knew that the USA could now defeat Japan without his help. This meant that Soviet forces wouldn't be needed in Japan, so the Soviets would not be able to extend their influence in East and Southeast Asia.

With Hitler now dead and Japan close to defeat, there was no common enemy for the USA and the USSR. This meant there was far less motivation for them to work together.

Outcomes of the Potsdam Conference

Important decisions were made at Potsdam about Germany:
- Its division into four zones (one each for the four major winners: the USA, Britain, France and the USSR) was finalised.
- Germany would pay reparations to the Allies, with most going to the USSR in the form of industrial equipment, such as machinery from factories.
- However, the three leaders disagreed strongly on how harshly to punish Germany. Stalin wanted to damage Germany, but the West wanted to avoid weakening Germany too severely.

There was also disagreement about how the new governments of countries in Eastern Europe would be decided. Stalin was reluctant to commit to holding free elections there, in case communist parties loyal to him lost.

Key word: atomic bomb

SOURCE B

This American cartoon was published on 11 August 1945, nine days after the Potsdam Conference ended. It suggests that the atomic bomb would affect all future peace negotiations because of its huge power. It certainly affected Truman and Stalin's ability to work together at Potsdam, even before it was used against Japan.

Work

1. Look back at all three conferences: Tehran, Yalta and Potsdam.
   a. Sum up the outcomes of each conference in no more than 30 words.
   b. Make a judgement about which one seems to have been the most successful and explain why.
   c. Make a judgement about the least successful and explain why.

2. Work in pairs. One of you will pretend to be part of the Soviet team at Potsdam, the other will be part of the American team. Write a short statement for the general public from your country's point of view, aiming for four to five sentences.

Exam-style question

Write a narrative account analysing the key developments in relations between the USA and the USSR between 1941 and 1945.

You **may** use the following in your answer:
- the Grand Alliance
- the Potsdam Conference

You **must** also use information of your own. (8 marks)

NAIL IT! As this question is worth 8 marks, you need to be selective about what you include. Think about a beginning, middle and end of the event, being careful to stick to the time frame given. Here you are exploring how and why the relationship changed from one of cooperation in 1941 to suspicion and disagreements by 1945.

Chapter 1: Early tensions between East and West

1.6 What was the impact of the atomic bomb?

Objectives
- Describe superpower relations in August 1945.
- Explain how tensions and suspicion increased over time.
- Evaluate the impact of the atomic bomb in increasing tensions.

While President Truman was meeting with the other leaders at the Potsdam Conference, back in the USA military scientists were running the final tests on the most destructive weapon ever created – the atomic bomb. The use of atomic bombs against Japan in August 1945 ended the Second World War but it had also increased tensions between the superpowers. What was the impact of the bomb on superpower relations?

A secret nuclear weapon?

Truman had been told about the atomic bomb as soon as he became president in April 1945. However, he made the decision not to tell his allies that this new bomb was nuclear – meaning that it gave out huge amounts of energy through reactions involving the splitting of atoms inside it. Despite this, Stalin was well aware of the bomb's existence, thanks to Soviet spies in the USA. The fact that Truman had not told Stalin added to the Soviets' growing view that the Americans simply could not be trusted.

The world's first atomic bomb was dropped on the Japanese city of Hiroshima on 6 August 1945, killing at least 70,000 people instantly. A second bomb was dropped on Nagasaki three days later, killing at least 40,000 instantly. Thousands more died in the days, weeks, months and even years that followed, as a result of the nuclear radiation poisoning that can damage the body's organs and blood, and can cause cancer. The Japanese use the word 'hibakusha' to describe a person who has become ill as a result of radiation sickness from the atomic bombs. They estimate there were over 650,000 hibakusha.

What was the impact of the atomic bomb on superpower relations?

Many historians argue that the dropping of the bombs in Japan marked the beginning of the Cold War, or was at least its first major event. By bringing an end to the USA's war against Japan, Truman was able to prevent the USSR from becoming involved. This in turn stopped the USSR claiming land in Asia, as it had already done in Eastern Europe. It also showed that the USA was determined to be the most powerful post-war country.

For Stalin and the Soviet Union, the bombs, and the secrecy surrounding them, confirmed the view that America could not be trusted. They also made it clear that the USA was now a potential threat, as well as a rival. Stalin made it his mission for the USSR to get its own atomic bomb. The alliance of the Second World War was well and truly over.

SOURCE A

The distinctive mushroom-shaped cloud that appeared after the second atomic bomb was dropped on Nagasaki in Japan on 9 August 1945

20 Part 1: The origins of the Cold War 1941–58

Mistrust and tensions increase – the two telegrams

As tensions increased in the weeks and months that followed, the two sides began to understand less about each other's actions, and became paranoid and mistrustful of each other. Official representatives, known as **diplomats**, in each country reported back on what they saw and gave their opinions on the governments. The two most important of these reports, sent by **telegram** (electronic signals through wires), were the Long Telegram and the Novikov Telegram.

- **The Long Telegram, February 1946** – George Kennan, the second in command of the USA Embassy in Moscow, sent an 8000-word telegram to the USA (telegrams were usually short messages, hence the name the 'Long' telegram). The message outlined his fears over the Soviet actions in Eastern Europe. He believed that the USSR was determined to spread its influence as far as possible and that it saw the USA as its enemy. He said that any attempt at cooperation between the countries was doomed to fail.
- **The Novikov Telegram, September 1946** – Nikolai Novikov, the Soviet Ambassador (senior diplomat) to the USA, sent his own telegram to the USSR stating his view that the USA was determined to dominate the world and spread its influence as far as possible. It said that the USA was economically powerful and should not be trusted.

Coming so soon after the atomic bombs, these two telegrams had a huge impact on shaping the two superpowers' ideas of each other.

Key words — diplomat | telegram

SOURCE B
A cartoon by the British cartoonist David Low, published in the London Evening Standard *newspaper, 30 October 1945*

"WHY CAN'T WE WORK TOGETHER IN MUTUAL TRUST & CONFIDENCE?"

INTERPRETATION C
From The Soviet Experiment *by American historian Ronald Grigor Suny, published in 1998*

> Stalin was dismayed that after all the Soviet sacrifices in the war to defeat Germany the American bomb had radically transformed the balance of world power. At a single stroke the huge Soviet conventional army was rendered far less powerful.

Work

1. When and where was the first atomic bomb dropped by the USA?
2. Look at **Source B**.
   a. What does the source show?
   b. What does it suggest about Truman and the potential consequences of his decision not to tell his allies about the atomic bomb?
3. Look at **Interpretation C**.
   a. What point is the historian making about the impact of the bomb?
   b. How far do you agree with this historian's view of the bomb's impact?

Exam-style question

Explain **two** consequences of the development of the atomic bomb in 1945. (8 marks)

NAIL IT! Remember to add detail to explain the consequence. For example, if you were to say that the atomic bomb led to an increase in tension between the superpowers, you would need to give specific examples of this, and you could say that it confirmed Soviet fears that the USA could not be trusted.

Chapter 1: Early tensions between East and West   21

1.7
The Iron Curtain descends

Objectives
- Describe how the Soviets created the 'satellite states' of Eastern Europe.
- Identify the concerns of the West.
- Explain why Churchill warned the USA about Soviet expansion.

Between 1945 and 1948, most countries in Eastern Europe came under the control of the USSR. After years of Nazi occupation, people found themselves living under another kind of dictatorship: communism. Soon it became clear that Europe was being split into two – separated by a so-called 'Iron Curtain'. What was the Iron Curtain? How did Stalin's actions in Europe create it? Why was this fast and effective takeover by the USSR such a threat to world peace?

The Soviets set up the satellite states, 1945–48

If Stalin had ordered his armies to set up new governments in Eastern European countries and kill all opponents outright, the people of Eastern Europe could have resisted, aided by the West. Instead, by allowing elections to take place in most countries and interfering with them, Stalin gradually ensured that enough people in the governments of these countries were communists, loyal to him. These countries then became the USSR's **satellite states**.

A
A map of Eastern Europe showing the satellite states of the USSR

Key
- Satellite states of the USSR, behind the Iron Curtain by 1948; sometimes referred to as the Eastern bloc
- Communist but not controlled by the USSR

① East Germany
Free elections didn't happen: the USSR helped a communist political party gain power.

② Poland
All the non-communist leaders in government were arrested or forced into exile (forced to leave the country). The results of an election in 1947 were tampered with, allowing a communist government to gain power.

③ Hungary
Stalin allowed elections. Although non-communist parties were more popular, Mátyás Rákosi, a pro-Soviet politician, had gained complete control by 1947 by using threats of Soviet invasion.

④ Romania
Stalin encouraged communist leaders to disrupt the government. The Soviet army intervened in 1945, creating a communist state.

⑤ Bulgaria
Communists interfered with the elections in 1945. All other parties were banned and their leaders were executed.

⑥ Czechoslovakia
In 1948, the USSR backed a communist armed takeover of the government. Non-communists were arrested and all other parties banned.

Part 1: The origins of the Cold War 1941–58

Key word | satellite state

INTERPRETATION B
Adapted from historian Anne Applebaum's 2012 book Iron Curtain

> The Soviet Union imported key elements of the Soviet system into every nation occupied by the Red Army. First … the Soviet NKVD [secret police and intelligence agency] created a secret police force … They used selective violence, carefully targeted their political enemies according to lists already put together … Secondly, in every occupied nation, Soviet authorities placed trusted local communists in charge of the era's most powerful form of mass media: the radio.

Churchill's 'Iron Curtain' speech

In early 1946, Truman invited Churchill (still a leading politician but not Prime Minister) to the USA to make a speech about what was going on in Europe. Churchill felt he had to warn the world about what the Soviets were doing in Eastern Europe.

SOURCE C
Adapted from Churchill's speech made at Fulton, Missouri, USA in March 1946

> An 'iron curtain' has descended across the continent. Behind that line lie all the capitals of the ancient states of Central and Eastern Europe. All these famous cities and the populations around them lie in what I must call the Soviet 'sphere', and all are subject not only to Soviet influence, but to a very high measure of control from Moscow [the capital of the USSR].

The main consequences of the Iron Curtain and the division of Europe

The creation of an Eastern bloc was a key reason for the start of the Cold War. However, the USA didn't want to risk a new war by intervening to stop Soviet expansion. You could argue that the West had allowed Stalin to create the Eastern bloc as a result of the agreements made at Tehran and Yalta, as well as with Churchill's 'percentages' deal in 1944.

By the time of Churchill's speech, it was clear that the Grand Alliance was well and truly over. The USA had committed itself to stopping the spread of communism in Europe by 1948, and came up with plans to do just that (known as the Truman Doctrine and Marshall Plan: these will be covered in Chapter 2).

Work

1. In your own words, describe what a satellite state was, giving one or two examples.
2. Study the boxes alongside map **A**. Create a flow diagram showing the steps the USSR took to create its satellite states. You could start like this: 'Step 1 – Ensure there are communists in the post-war governments.'
3. Stalin wrote a response to Churchill's 'Iron Curtain' speech in a Soviet newspaper. What points do you think he might have made to defend the takeover of Eastern Europe?

Meanwhile…

The British economy was under huge strain as it struggled to recover from the cost of the Second World War. For example, rationing of certain foods continued until the mid-1950s and Britain received a significant amount of money from Marshall Aid (see page 26). As a result, the British could no longer afford to take a leading role in world affairs and played a far smaller part in the Cold War than the USA. Churchill – still a leading politician but not Prime Minister – was frustrated by this.

Exam-style question

Write a narrative account analysing the key events at the beginning of the Cold War (1945–46).

You **may** use the following in your answer:
- the Potsdam Conference
- Churchill's 'Iron Curtain' speech

You **must** also use information of your own. (8 marks)

NAIL IT! As well as a clear beginning, middle and end, your answer needs to make links between events and explain them clearly. Analyse why one side acted as they did, and how this provoked a response from the other side. What were the decision-makers trying to achieve?

Chapter 1: Early tensions between East and West

2.1 Containing communism: what was the Truman Doctrine?

Objectives
- Describe the key features of the Truman Doctrine.
- Assess its impact on superpower relations.

When Harry Truman became US president in April 1945, he had little experience or knowledge of international issues. Yet he found himself dealing with an increasingly complicated and tense world. In the years after the Second World War, Truman had to deal with the Soviet Union and its expansion into Eastern Europe. His answer was the Truman Doctrine, a political approach that would guide American policy for many years to come. What was the Truman Doctrine? Why and how did it develop? What was the USSR's response?

Containing communism

On 12 March 1947, with the Soviet Union occupying Eastern Europe and looking to make its influence there permanent, Harry Truman delivered the most important speech of his presidency. Speaking to the **US Congress** – the part of the US government that makes laws – Truman talked about the threat posed by communism and made clear his determination to stop it from spreading further around the world. He promised to support, in whatever way necessary, any country that was under threat of becoming communist. He accepted that it was too late to do this in many parts of Eastern Europe but promised to stop communism from going beyond these countries. This idea became known as **containment** because it involved 'containing' communism.

SOURCE A
An extract from Truman's speech, March 1947

> At the present moment in world history nearly every nation must choose between alternative ways of life – the choice is often not a free one. One way of life is based on the will of the majority, free elections, freedom of speech and religion. The second way of life is based upon the will of the minority forcing themselves onto the majority; it relies on terror, a controlled press and radio, fixed elections, and a lack of personal freedom. I believe the United States must support people who are trying to resist being enslaved by armed minorities or by outside pressures.

Meanwhile…

Although Truman's speech was a response to the general situation in Europe, it was events in Greece that really pushed him into action. Greece was in the grip of a civil war between communists and supporters of the former king, and it flared up again in 1946. The Americans did not want Greece to be communist and so needed the communists to be defeated. Initially Britain funded the anti-communist groups, but this could not last. The USA needed to help too.

Later on…

Truman's 1947 speech became known as the Truman Doctrine. A **doctrine** is a belief or set of beliefs held and taught by a group or organisation. The Truman Doctrine became a metaphor for aid to keep a nation free from communist influence.

Later on…

Fears about the spread of communism developed further under Truman's successor as president, Dwight Eisenhower, with the development of the 'domino theory': if one country became communist, this would lead to all its neighbouring countries becoming communist too. The USA was particularly worried about this happening in East and Southeast Asia, which explains why it adopted a policy of containment and got involved in countries where communism was taking hold, such as Korea and Vietnam in the 1950s.

Key words | US Congress | containment | doctrine | Cominform

Harry S. Truman

- Became US vice president in January 1945 and then president just three months later, following the death of Franklin Roosevelt.
- As president in the final months of the Second World War, he made many important decisions (including the bombing of Hiroshima and Nagasaki) and took part in negotiations at Potsdam.
- He shaped US policy through the Truman Doctrine and made the decision to become involved in the Korean War in 1950.
- He left the role of president in 1952, having decided not to stand for re-election.

The Soviet response: Cominform

In response to Truman's speech, Stalin created the Communist Information Bureau, or **Cominform**. The idea was to bring together communist countries in Eastern Europe into one group to ensure that they followed the same policies. Stalin knew the Truman Doctrine was a threat to the spread of communism in Europe and wanted to take tighter control over Eastern European countries.

SOURCE B

A cartoon from the British magazine Punch, *which used humour to criticise events, people and ideas, published in June 1947. The bus conductor on the left is Truman and the one on the right is Stalin.*

Work

1. Explain what is meant by 'containing' communism. You may find it useful to refer to **Source A** in your answer.
2. Why did Stalin create Cominform?
3. Look at **Source B**.
   a. What can you see in this source?
   b. How does this source reflect the events of 1947?
   c. Are there any differences between the ways Stalin and Truman are behaving? What might this tell you about the cartoonist's point of view?
4. 'The Truman Doctrine increased tensions between the superpowers.' How far do you agree?

Exam-style question

Explain **two** consequences of the Truman Doctrine. (8 marks)

NAIL IT! Remember to use words and phrases that show what happened, including 'This led to...' and 'As a result of...'. For example: 'Stalin saw the Truman Doctrine as a clear threat to the USSR's influence. *This led to* the creation of Cominform in response.'

Chapter 2: The development of the Cold War

2.2 What was the Marshall Plan?

Objectives
- Describe the features of the Marshall Plan.
- Examine the purpose of the plan.
- Assess how it reflected the Truman Doctrine.

The Second World War had devastated Europe. Millions of people had died and countries across the continent lay in ruins. In 1947, the US government launched a recovery plan designed to get Europe back on its feet by providing the resources needed for countries to rebuild. The plan, known as the Marshall Plan, would be available to every country, including those east of the Iron Curtain. What were the aims of the Marshall Plan? How did it work? How did it relate to the Truman Doctrine and the wider US policy in Europe?

A devastated continent

The situation across Europe after the Second World War was one that greatly concerned the American government. Countries had been left devastated by the fighting and even the victorious nations, such as Britain and France, were nearly bankrupt. The US government knew full well that when people were left in poverty and with a feeling of hopelessness about the future they often turned to extreme political ideas. For this reason, the USA saw Europe as vulnerable to communism.

The European Recovery Plan (nicknamed the **Marshall Plan** after **US Secretary of State** George Marshall, the politician who planned and coordinated it) aimed to provide economic support to countries in order for them to rebuild quickly. Although communism was a concern, it was not Marshall's only consideration. While the USA had come out of the war with a strong economy, this would only last if there was a strong Europe to trade with. Marshall made it clear to any countries receiving money (known as 'aid') that they had to spend part of it on US goods, such as food and farm machinery.

> **Meanwhile...**
>
> In October 1949, there was a communist revolution in China. In the coming decades this would have a huge impact on the Cold War as the People's Republic of China sought to increase its own power and influence in the world.

The Marshall Plan

The Marshall Plan had a number of key aims:
- to enable a quick economic recovery in Europe, making communism less attractive
- to encourage European countries to work together, and with the USA
- to create a market for American goods and help the US economy.

The amount of aid given to each country through the Marshall Plan

Country	Amount of aid
UK	$3.2b
France	$2.7b
Italy	$1.5b
West Germany	$1.4b
Netherlands	$1.1b
Greece	$694m
Austria	$677m
Belgium/Luxembourg	$556m
Denmark	$271m
Norway	$254m
Turkey	$221m
Ireland	$146m
Sweden	$107m
Portugal	$50m
Iceland	$29m

| Key words | Marshall Plan | US Secretary of State |

Was the plan successful?

Aid provided by the Marshall Plan played a very important role in Western Europe's recovery from the Second World War, allowing many countries to recover much more quickly than they would have done on their own. The impact on the American economy was also important, as the USA now had more trading partners in Europe. Most importantly, the Marshall Plan showed that the USA was committed to being involved in Europe for the long term – a clear message to the USSR.

The plan also achieved the aim of preventing communism in Western Europe, although communist parties did continue to exist there. In addition, Marshall Aid brought Western European countries together, and they remained loyal to the USA for the remainder of the Cold War. However, a sense of unity was also created between those countries on the other side of the Iron Curtain, all of which turned down the support offered by the plan.

Meanwhile…

Following the Marshall Plan in Europe, the US government began to take a similar approach in other parts of the world. In what became known as the Point Four Program (named because it was point 4 in the foreign policy section of the speech Truman made after he was re-elected as president in 1949), the USA provided money and support to developing countries around the world. As with the Marshall Plan, part of the aim was to prevent these countries from falling under communist influence.

SOURCE B
Parade to mark the Marshall Plan's millionth ton of food for Greece, bought using Marshall Aid, 1947

SOURCE C
A cartoon by the American cartoonist D. R. Fitzpatrick, entitled 'The Way Back' and published in 1947. The rope says 'The Marshall Plan'.

Work

1. Explain what the Marshall Plan was in your own words.

2. Look at **Source B**.
   a. Describe what is happening in the source.
   b. How can this photograph be seen as evidence that the Marshall Plan achieved its aims?

3. Look at **Source C**.
   a. Describe what you can see in this source.
   b. Explain how this source shows the reasons behind the Marshall Plan. To help, think about what the man is pulling himself up from.

4. How far should the USA have seen the Marshall Plan as a success?

Exam-style question

Write a narrative account analysing the key events surrounding the introduction of Marshall Aid in 1948.

You **may** use the following in your answer:
- Truman Doctrine
- arrival of American farming equipment in Europe

You **must** also use information of your own. (8 marks)

Chapter 2: The development of the Cold War   27

2.3 How did the USSR respond to the Marshall Plan?

Objectives
- Examine the Soviet response to the Marshall Plan.
- Explain how this led to the creation of Comecon.
- Analyse the impact of these plans on superpower relations.

For the countries of Western Europe, the Marshall Plan played a vital role in their recovery from the devastation of war. In Eastern Europe, however, it was a different story. On the clear instructions of Stalin, no country behind the Iron Curtain accepted any support. The Soviets established an alternative plan called Comecon – and once again a clear division had been drawn. Why was Stalin so opposed to the Marshall Plan? What was Comecon and how did it work? How did the rival recovery plans affect superpower relations?

'Dollar imperialism'

In Stalin's mind there was no doubt about the purpose behind Marshall Aid (the aid delivered by the Marshall Plan): the USA wanted to buy influence in Europe. It was seen by the Soviets as an example of '**dollar imperialism**' – the USA using its wealth to build its power and secure capitalism. Stalin believed that any country that accepted Marshall Aid would be loyal to the USA in the future. This meant that he simply could not allow any countries behind the Iron Curtain to accept aid.

Comecon

Having made it clear that Eastern European countries should not accept Marshall Aid, Stalin needed to create an alternative way of offering support. Just as in Western Europe, these countries had been devastated by war and needed help to recover. In 1949, Stalin created **Comecon** (the Council for Mutual Economic Assistance). The scheme was different from the Marshall Plan in that it involved countries working together to help each other rebuild, rather than one country providing money. It was supposed to be a group of equal partners, but in reality it was tightly controlled by the Soviet government in Moscow.

SOURCE B

A Soviet image by Alexander Zhitomirsky, published in 1947

INTERPRETATION A

Adapted from *Phantom Spies, Phantom Justice* by Miriam Moskowitz, published in 2010. Moskowitz was an American schoolteacher who served two years in prison for lying to protect Soviet spies in 1950. She maintained her innocence until her death in 2018.

> Since the Marshall Plan demanded the opening up of European markets to America, the Soviet Union saw it as a hostile, predatory manoeuvre and declined to participate. It also loudly criticised it. On the other hand, the Plan's anti-Soviet nature was barely concealed.

Meanwhile...

Although closely related, Cominform and Comecon had different roles. The purpose of Cominform was to ensure unity between communist countries, whereas Comecon aimed to rebuild the countries following the devastation of war.

Key words | dollar imperialism | Comecon

What was the impact of Marshall Aid and Comecon?

The two separate recovery plans further divided Europe into two camps. They secured the influence of the two superpowers over the two sides of Europe. Neither side trusted the motives of the other and this led to greater tension and paranoia in the months and years that followed.

SOURCE C

A cartoon from the Soviet magazine Krokodil, published in July 1950. The caption was 'Peace is excluded from paradise.' The American police officer and other westerners are chasing peace out of Europe because of the Marshall Plan.

Meanwhile…

Despite being a Communist country, Yugoslavia's relationship with the USSR was unique. As the Soviets had not occupied it after the Second World War, its leader, General Tito, had no particular loyalty to Stalin. When Tito accepted Marshall Aid in 1948, Yugoslavia was expelled from Cominform and became the only independent communist country in Europe – and the only one outside the Iron Curtain. This situation remained until the early 1990s when it broke up into several smaller countries including Bosnia, Serbia and Croatia.

Meanwhile…

As events unfolded in Europe, other parts of the world saw increased interest in communism, something that greatly concerned the US government. In South America, there was growing support for communist groups. For example, in Guatemala, communist politicians were elected and, in the 1950s, took land from wealthy businesses and gave it to poor farmers. Fearing the spread of communism, the US government supported a group of rebels to overthrow the elected government and replace it with a strongly anti-communist one in 1954.

Work

1. Look at **Source B**.
   a. What can you see in this image? Think about what is on the plate and what the person's face is.
   b. What does the source tell you about how the USSR viewed the Marshall Plan? Think about what it is suggesting the USA is trying to do.

2. Read **Interpretation A**.
   a. In your own words, explain what the interpretation is saying about the Marshall Plan and the Soviet response.
   b. How far do you agree with the interpretation that the Marshall Plan was a 'hostile, predatory manoeuvre'?

3. Look at **Source C**. What is happening in this source, and what can you learn from it about the Soviet view of the Marshall Plan?

4. Explain what Comecon was, and how it was different from Marshall Aid.

Exam-style question

Explain the following:

The importance of the Marshall Plan for increased tensions between the superpowers by 1948.   (8 marks)

NAIL IT! This question is asking you to write about increased tensions. You could write about how the Marshall Plan was viewed by the USSR, or about the creation of Comecon, but remember to relate everything you write about back to the question.

Chapter 2: The development of the Cold War

2.4 Berlin divided

Objectives
- Describe the division of Germany and Berlin into four zones after 1945.
- Identify the key differences between West Germany and East Germany.
- Explain why West Berlin contributed to early tension in the Cold War.

At the end of the war, Germany was divided into four zones, each one controlled by one of the four major winning countries – the USA, Britain, France and the USSR. It was also decided that Berlin, Germany's capital, should be divided. Berlin was actually within the Soviet area of Germany, but was still divided between the USA, Britain, France and the USSR. Why were Germany and Berlin divided in this way? How were the areas controlled? How did this division increase tension at the start of the Cold War?

Post-war Germany: under occupation

The British, French, Americans and Soviets had fought their way across Europe to defeat Hitler. At the Yalta and Potsdam conferences, the Big Three were able to agree that Germany should be split into four zones once the war was won. These would be occupied by Allied troops, helping to set up new governments and dealing with the aftermath of war.

In each zone, the job of rebuilding Germany from its ruins was huge. Many towns and cities had been destroyed by Allied bombing. Fierce fighting between Nazi and Soviet soldiers had taken place on the streets of eastern Germany. However, the Allies had other motives as well as simply helping the German people to recover.

The division and occupation of Germany was supposed to be temporary until a new, stable and peaceful government could be formed. However, the division lasted until 1990.

> **Meanwhile...**
>
> France wasn't part of the Big Three, but the French leader Charles de Gaulle insisted that France should have a key role in post-war Europe. Although de Gaulle wasn't well-liked by the Big Three, they were happy to allow France to take on the burden of running a sector in Germany. Stalin insisted that the French zone be carved out of the American and British zones that had already been planned. For practical reasons, the French sector was next to the border with France.

SOURCE B

German women carried out much of the work of clearing the streets of rubble caused by wartime destruction, earning the nickname 'Trummelfrauen' (rubble women). Here some Trummelfrauen are clearing rubble in front of the seriously damaged Reichstag (Parliament) building in Berlin, 1948.

A
The division of Germany as agreed at the Yalta and Potsdam conferences in 1945

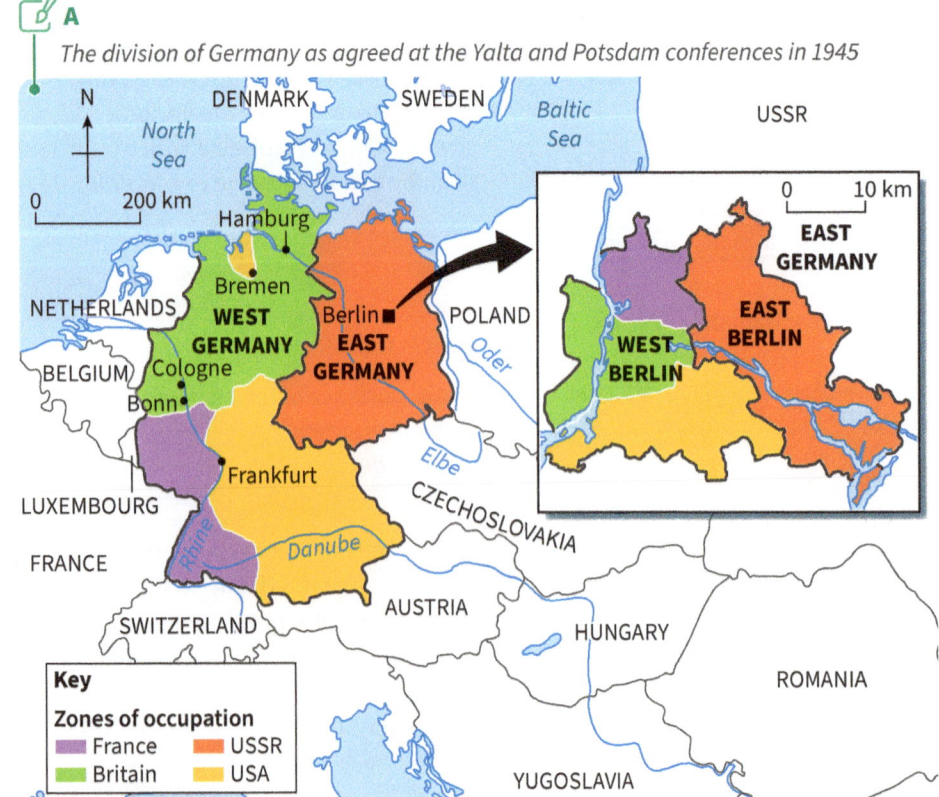

Part 1: The origins of the Cold War 1941–58

Four zones in Germany and Berlin

The three Western zones were run by the USA, France and Britain. The differences between how the West ran West Germany and how the Soviets ran the East grew more obvious as time went on. The West invested large sums of money into the industries of their sectors (for example, spending money to rebuild West German factories), partly so they could trade with West Germany.

By contrast, Stalin was still determined to take reparations from Germany. Large amounts of industrial equipment were seized from the Soviet zone and taken to the USSR – whole factories were even dismantled and taken away. Like all Eastern bloc countries, East Germany's economy was now set up on communist principles. These two factors meant that living standards for most people in East Germany were much lower than in West Germany.

Politically, the difference between the zones was also very clear. East Germany became a dictatorship with the USSR strongly involved in government decisions. A secret police force known as the Stasi was formed. Their job was to watch the population for any sign of rebellion. There was no freedom of speech, the press was censored and culture was strictly controlled.

SOURCE C

This sign, in post-war Berlin, became symbolic of divisions not just within Berlin, but Europe as a whole

West Berlin: 'a capitalist island in a sea of communism'

Meanwhile, the USA saw an opportunity to use West Germany – and especially West Berlin – as a way to make communism look like a terrible system. It was no accident that West Germany received the fourth-largest amount of Marshall Aid (after the UK, France and Italy). A huge amount of money was spent on quickly rebuilding West Berlin in particular, and making sure that living standards were high. This made capitalism and democracy look like better ways to run a country.

West Berlin's success angered Stalin. As it was located in the middle of East Germany, it was obvious to many in the Soviet zone that things were improving faster under capitalism. At the conferences in 1945, the Big Three had agreed to cooperate on the running of their zones. Any major decisions should have been discussed beforehand. But by 1947, the British, Americans and French began meeting to discuss Germany without a Soviet representative being there. Before long, Stalin decided to take action to try to get all of Berlin under Soviet control.

Work

1. Imagine you are writing a travel guide to Berlin in 1947.
   a. Describe the differences between West and East Berlin.
   b. What advice would you give to your readers when staying in East Berlin and in West Berlin?

2. It was Churchill who described West Berlin as 'a capitalist island in a sea of communism'. What do you think he meant by this? Explain it in your own words, making sure you include plenty of contextual knowledge.

Exam-style question

Explain the following:

The importance of the Potsdam Conference (1945) for the beginning of the Cold War between the USA and the USSR. (8 marks)

NAIL IT! Now you've studied the division of Berlin, you could discuss the consequences of the decision to divide Berlin that was made at the Potsdam Conference (see pages 18–19).

Chapter 2: The development of the Cold War

2.5 The Berlin Crisis: Stalin's blockade

Objectives
- Identify the changes the Western allies were making to their sectors of Berlin.
- Explain why Stalin ordered the blockade of West Berlin.
- Describe the nature of the Berlin blockade.

On 24 June 1948, a crisis swept through Berlin. Suddenly, all access routes by land and water into West Berlin were blocked on Stalin's orders. West Berliners found themselves cut off from Western Europe: the Berlin blockade had begun. Why did Stalin take such aggressive action?

The build-up to the Berlin Crisis

The USA, Britain, France and the USSR had agreed at the Potsdam Conference how to split Berlin. However, in London in January 1947, the USA and Britain met and agreed to merge their two zones of Germany and Berlin together, creating a larger zone called Bizonia (which later became Trizonia when France merged its zone in April 1949).

Stalin had not been consulted about the creation of Bizonia. No Soviet representatives were at the January 1947 meeting and they were not given any information about it later. Stalin accused the West of going behind his back over the running of Germany.

Before long, Marshall Aid was rapidly improving living standards in West Berlin. The wealthier capitalist half of the city was visible to East Berliners, making communism look like a bad system.

The trigger: a new currency

Creating Bizonia gave the West another opportunity to weaken Soviet influence in Germany. On 23 June 1948, the British and Americans introduced a new currency in Bizonia: the Deutsche Mark. People immediately trusted this new money, which was seen as more valuable than the old currency, the Reichsmark. As a result, many East Germans rushed to exchange their East German currency for the new Deutsche Mark. This rapidly decreased the value of the East German currency, which was a big threat to the economy. Stalin was furious. He decided to take action, starting the Berlin Crisis with a **blockade** to cut West Berlin off from the West.

A
Berlin was divided into four zones: East Berlin and the three zones of West Berlin. In early 1949, the USA and Britain merged their zones.

SOURCE B
In June 1948, Berliners from the Soviet zone immediately rushed to exchange their East German currency for the new Deutsche Mark introduced by the West. You can see them waiting in line in this photograph.

32 Part 1: The origins of the Cold War 1941–58

Key words | blockade | consumer goods

> **Long-term reasons for the blockade**
> - West Berlin's position in East Germany, an 'island in a sea of communism'.
> - With investment from the West, West Berlin recovered much faster than East Berlin, which was obvious to East Germans.
> - Stalin, meanwhile, was determined to make East Germany pay for the devastation of the Second World War.
> - Stalin became desperate to force the West out of Berlin.

> **Medium-term reasons for the blockade**
> - The USA and Britain merged their sectors into one zone called Bizonia in January 1947. Stalin was not consulted on this.
> - Marshall Aid was approved by the US Congress in March 1948.
> - The Soviets began monitoring all road and rail traffic into Berlin.

> **Short-term reasons for the blockade**
> - The USA and Britain introduced a new, more valuable currency in Bizonia on 23 June 1948.
> - East Germans rushed to convert their money, seriously undermining East Germany's economy.

The Berlin blockade: what was it?

Most goods and supplies into West Berlin had to get through part of East Germany first. This gave Stalin the opportunity to take action against the West. By blocking the road, canal and rail routes from West Germany to West Berlin, he could make life extremely difficult for West Berliners. Not only was there a risk that they would run out of the **consumer goods** that weren't available in East Germany, but they could also run out of basic essentials like food and coal as these were delivered by lorry and train. The blockade prevented any more Marshall Aid from reaching West Berlin.

The blockade, which began on 24 June 1948, was an aggressive move by Stalin, but stopped short of being a declaration of war against the West. His main objective in ordering the Berlin blockade was to force the West to abandon West Berlin, allowing it to become Soviet-dominated. He expected West Berliners to face starvation – forcing the USA, Britain and France to give in or risk people dying. However, he severely underestimated the West's commitment to keeping its influence over the German capital.

> **Work**
>
> 1. In your own words, describe what a blockade is, *or* create a diagram showing a blockade.
> 2. In 50 words or fewer, explain why Stalin ordered the Berlin blockade.
> 3. Which side do you think was more to blame for the Berlin Crisis? Create a table, with the reasons the West can be blamed in one column and the reasons the Soviets can be blamed in one column, and then come to a judgement. When considering the reasons for blame, think back to the Yalta Conference in 1945.

> **Later on…**
>
> The Berlin Wall, separating East and West Berlin, was built in 1961. Make sure you don't confuse the Berlin blockade in 1948–49 with the Berlin Wall!

> **Exam-style question**
>
> Explain the following:
>
> The importance of the 1945 conferences for the start of the Berlin Crisis in 1948. (8 marks)

> **NAIL IT!** Think about what happened at the 1945 conferences and then think about how important what happened was for the development of the Berlin Crisis. You must link events at the 1945 conferences with the Berlin Crisis to answer the question successfully.

Chapter 2: The development of the Cold War 33

2.6 The Berlin Crisis: the airlift and its impact

Objectives
- Explain why the West refused to give up on West Berlin.
- Describe key features of the airlift into West Berlin.
- Explain Stalin's response to the airlift and its impact on the Cold War.

Determined not to abandon West Berlin to the Soviets, the West decided to fly food and fuel into West Berlin and – after a few months – was transporting over 4,000 tonnes of supplies there every day. The airlift meant that the blockade didn't have the effect that Stalin had hoped and it was eventually called off. But how did the Berlin Crisis of 1948–49 further deepen the Cold War divide?

'If Berlin falls, West Germany will be next'

This was a remark by General Clay, the US commander in West Berlin. He believed giving in to Stalin would be allowing communism to spread even further. The West also felt that it couldn't let West Berliners down, so allowing the city to fall to the Soviets was simply not an option.

The West could have chosen to go to war over the blockade, invading East Germany. Although the USA still had the advantage of being the only superpower with nuclear weapons, this option could have caused terrible casualties and devastation.

A third option was to continue to supply West Berlin by air. The situation was critical: West Berliners only had around six weeks' worth of food and fuel left.

Key features of the Berlin airlift

Stalin had cut off access to West Berlin through East Germany, but there were three agreed air 'corridors' over East Germany into Berlin, one for each of the Western allies to reach their sectors. Britain and the USA began the airlift on 26 June 1948, with the support of France and other allies.

Within a few weeks the airlift had become very efficient and soon planes were landing in West Berlin every three minutes, day and night. By the end of the airlift, over 2 million tonnes of supplies had reached West Berlin. This was only just enough for its residents to keep going: they suffered real hardship while the blockade continued.

Stalin's reaction

The airlift deeply frustrated Stalin, but there was little he could do. He did order the East German authorities to disrupt the pilots by shining searchlights at night to dazzle their vision, and several people were killed when planes crashed.

Stalin increased pressure on the West Berliners by cutting off their electricity. He offered them extra supplies if they moved to East Germany. Despite the severe shortages West Berliners faced, only two per cent took up Stalin's offer and moved to the East. By spring 1949, it was clear that the blockade had failed, and in May Stalin called it off.

 SOURCE A

Traute Grier, a young girl living in West Berlin during the blockade, later described how difficult it was.

> I remember how [my mother] used to save her food and biscuits for me … regardless of how empty her own stomach was. Sometimes she even collapsed – that's how malnourished she was … At home we had to carefully plan when we would cook, as we only had electricity at certain times. As a result, it was not unusual that my mother would get up in the middle of the night at 2am and start boiling some potatoes.

Key word | airlift

SOURCE B

One of the Western planes flying over Berlin children in 1948. As well as supplying West Berliners with the essentials, the West also saw a propaganda opportunity with the airlift. Planes sometimes dropped sweets too, ensuring that children appreciated what the Western allies were doing!

SOURCE C

A cartoon from the British magazine Punch, *which poked fun at current events. It shows a frustrated Stalin watching the airlift, depicted by birds carrying food and coal. Stalin is holding a gun, which suggests that, in July 1948 (when the cartoon was created), many people were worried that Stalin would use his armed forces to stop the airlift and provoke all-out war. However, this didn't happen as the risk was too great for the USSR.*

Work

1. **a** Make a table with two columns. In the first column, list all the actions the Soviets took during the Berlin Crisis. In the other column, list all the actions the West took. Try to be as specific as possible, and keep them in the correct chronological order.
   b Now use arrows to show in your list which actions were responses to something the other side had done.

Exam-style question

Write a narrative account analysing the key events of the Berlin Crisis (1948–49).

You **may** use the following in your answer:
- Stalin's fears
- the airlift

You **must** also use information of your own. (8 marks)

NAIL IT! It's important to think about the level of detail to include about each event in your narrative account. For example, for this question, avoid going into too much detail about why Stalin ordered the blockade. Quickly explain Stalin's fears, then move on to what happened next.

Key consequences of the Berlin Crisis

The airlift showed the determination of the West not to abandon West Berlin. It also increased fears of Soviet aggression, which led some countries in the West to consider forming NATO, a new military alliance (see pages 38–39). The West Berliners themselves had also become defiant. They had put up with real hardship in order to remain part of the West.

There was now no hope of a united Germany. The Berlin Crisis led to a formal, more permanent division of the country and the sectors were renamed. Bizonia joined up with the French sector and became the Federal Republic of Germany (FRG), and East Germany was renamed the German Democratic Republic (GDR). Berlin remained a strong focus of superpower tension well into the 1960s, and a symbol of the division between East and West until the end of the Cold War.

Chapter 2: The development of the Cold War

3.1 The arms race

Objectives
- Describe the arms race and how it developed over time.
- Analyse the consequences of the arms race for superpower relations and the wider world.

The USA's development of the atomic bomb in 1945 kickstarted an arms race in which the two sides tried to have more powerful weapons than their rival. This ran throughout the Cold War. As the world looked on in fear, each side was determined to be ahead in the development of more powerful nuclear weapons – with enough to destroy the world and wipe out humanity several times over. How did the arms race develop over time? What was its impact on superpower relations? How close did the world really come to total destruction?

The beginning of the nuclear age

Following the atomic bombings of Hiroshima and Nagasaki in 1945, Stalin was determined to match the USA's strength in nuclear weapons. This was achieved on 29 August 1949, when the Soviets successfully tested their own A-bomb (atomic bomb). Having lost the advantage, President Truman quickly ordered work to begin on an even more powerful bomb.

The first **hydrogen bomb** – a more advanced version of an atomic bomb – was tested by the USA in 1952. The USSR had its own version a year later. In 1961, the USSR detonated the most powerful bomb the world has ever seen. Known as the 'Tsar bomb', the explosion was more powerful than all of the explosives used during the Second World War combined! In the years that followed, both sides continued to spend vast sums of money on developing new and more powerful nuclear weapons, terrified that the other side may get ahead in this race.

Mutually Assured Destruction – a world on the edge

Despite the huge number of weapons on both sides, not a single nuclear weapon was launched during the Cold War. This was largely due to the idea of Mutually Assured Destruction (MAD): both sides knew that if any weapon was launched, the other side would respond and retaliate, meaning both sides – and most of the world – would be destroyed.

Despite this, there were a number of occasions when nuclear war looked possible, or even likely. The most notable was in 1962, during the Cuban Missile Crisis (see pages 58–61). During these moments of high tension, governments around the world came up with plans to prepare for nuclear war and gave people advice about what to do if it happened. In reality, these plans were just to reassure people – in a nuclear attack, there would be little that anyone could do.

> **Later on...**
>
> Although the USA and the USSR were the first countries to develop nuclear weapons, they were not the only ones. Britain became a nuclear power in 1952, and was followed by France (1960) and China (1964). India became the sixth country to hold nuclear weapons, in 1974. More recently, in 1998, Pakistan announced that it possessed nuclear weapons, although it is widely believed that it had had them for sometime before this. Most recently, in 2006, North Korea successfully tested a nuclear weapon. These eight countries, along with Israel (which is widely believed to hold nuclear weapons despite never having officially stated that it does), make up the nuclear powers of today.

SOURCE A

Children in a New York school practising for a nuclear attack with a 'duck and cover' drill in 1962

Part 1: The origins of the Cold War 1941–58

Key word | hydrogen bomb/H-bomb

The space race

Alongside – and very much linked to – the arms race was the space race. From the 1950s onwards both superpowers tried to beat each other in putting satellites and then human beings into space. The USSR had the upper hand early, when it launched the first satellite (Sputnik) into orbit in 1957 and then the first human (Yuri Gagarin, in a spacecraft called Vostok I) in 1961. Over the two decades that followed each side achieved a number of incredible firsts, including the USA sending the first humans to the Moon, in 1969. The space race was about showing superiority in technology, but it was also about weapons. The technology to launch rockets into space was the same as that used to launch nuclear weapons.

SOURCE B

Soviet engineer Valentina Tereshkova, the first woman in space, 16 June 1963

Slowly stepping back from the edge

Following the Cuban Missile Crisis in 1962 (see pages 58–61), there was a shift in thinking. While the arms race did not stop, it did slow down as the two sides recognised that it could not continue. They knew that there was the possibility of a mistake or misunderstanding leading to nuclear war. In the 1980s, tensions rose again and spending on arms started to increase. The presence of nuclear weapons throughout the Cold War made all moments of tension a serious concern for the whole of humanity.

SOURCE C

Adapted from the Russell-Einstein Manifesto, a joint statement made in July 1955 by the writer Bertrand Russell and the physicist Albert Einstein, two of the most respected people of their time.

No doubt, in an H-bomb war, great cities would be obliterated … but we now know, especially that nuclear bombs can gradually spread destruction over a very much wider area than had been supposed.

It is stated on very good authority that a bomb can now be manufactured which will be 2,500 times as powerful as that which destroyed Hiroshima. Such a bomb, if exploded near the ground or under water, sends radio-active particles into the upper air. They sink gradually and reach the surface of the earth in the form of a deadly dust or rain. The best authorities are unanimous in saying that a war with H-bombs might possibly put an end to the human race.

Work

1. Create a short timeline showing the early years of the arms race. You could also include some key events from the space race.
2. Explain the idea of Mutually Assured Destruction.
3. Look at **Source A**. Why do you think countries issued advice like 'duck and cover', when they knew it would be of little help?
4. Look at **Source C**.
   a. In your own words, summarise the point that Russell and Einstein are making.
   b. Why do you think the arms race continued, despite this view being held by two such respected figures?

Exam-style question

Explain the following:

The importance of the arms race for increasing superpower tension up to 1960. (8 marks)

NAIL IT! Make sure you look carefully at the date or dates in the question. This one only goes up to 1960, which means you can include the early arms race and space race but nothing beyond this date!

Chapter 3: The Cold War intensifies

3.2 NATO and the Warsaw Pact: new alliances

Objectives
- Explain why Western European countries wanted an alliance with the USA.
- Describe the Soviet response to NATO and the creation of the Warsaw Pact.

The Berlin blockade sent a warning to the West. It was clear that the USSR wanted to maintain and even expand its influence over the satellite states. In 1949, NATO – the North Atlantic Treaty Organization – was set up to provide Western Europe with military protection by the USA. The USSR responded by setting up the Warsaw Pact, to rival NATO. What were the aims of NATO and the Warsaw Pact? Who joined? What impact did these new alliances have on the Cold War?

Why was NATO formed in 1949?

Many Western European leaders felt they would be unable to defend their countries against attack by the USSR. The British Foreign Secretary, Ernest Bevin, suggested that the Western European nations should form a defensive alliance, backed by the USA.

Soon after the Berlin airlift began, Bevin discussed the idea with the USA and, in April 1949, the North Atlantic Treaty Organization (NATO) was created.

NATO membership

The USA, Britain and France were among the original 12 NATO members. Greece and Turkey joined in 1952. Being part of NATO often meant countries agreeing to have a permanent US military base on their soil. Members also agreed to go to war to defend each other if they were threatened by the USSR.

Although there were never enough NATO soldiers to outnumber Red Army troops, it was meant to make Stalin think twice about further action threatening the West. The USA promised military aid if any NATO states were directly threatened by the East.

SOURCE A

This cartoon was published in a British newspaper in April 1949, soon after NATO was formed. The figure shown is Stalin, and the 'Atlantic Pact' was another way of referring to NATO. The words on Stalin's bag say 'FEAR' and 'SUSPICION'.

Stalin's reaction

Stalin was outraged by the formation of NATO. He believed it was part of a plan to attack the Eastern bloc in the future. Nevertheless, Stalin didn't respond with the creation of his own military alliance – this didn't happen until after he died in 1953 and Nikita Khrushchev became Soviet leader.

The creation of the Warsaw Pact

The East was deeply suspicious of NATO. When West Germany joined NATO in 1955, it was agreed that there would be a US military base in West Germany, close to the Iron Curtain. This worried the leaders of the USSR and the satellite states, and so they formed their own military alliance. It was called the Treaty of Friendship, Cooperation and Mutual Assistance. However, it became known as the Warsaw Pact because it was agreed and signed in the Polish capital, Warsaw. The Warsaw Pact had eight members, including the USSR and East Germany. Members had to agree to keep their governments communist.

Meanwhile...

1949 was a significant year for China too. After years of civil war and revolution, China became communist under the leadership of Chairman Mao Zedong. The West feared that China and the USSR, with their very large populations, would form a communist superbloc. However, Mao fell out with the new Soviet leader, Khrushchev, so China and the USSR rarely cooperated with each other.

Part 1: The origins of the Cold War 1941–58

B

The location of NATO and Warsaw Pact countries in Europe by the end of 1955

Key
- Warsaw Pact
- NATO
- The Iron Curtain

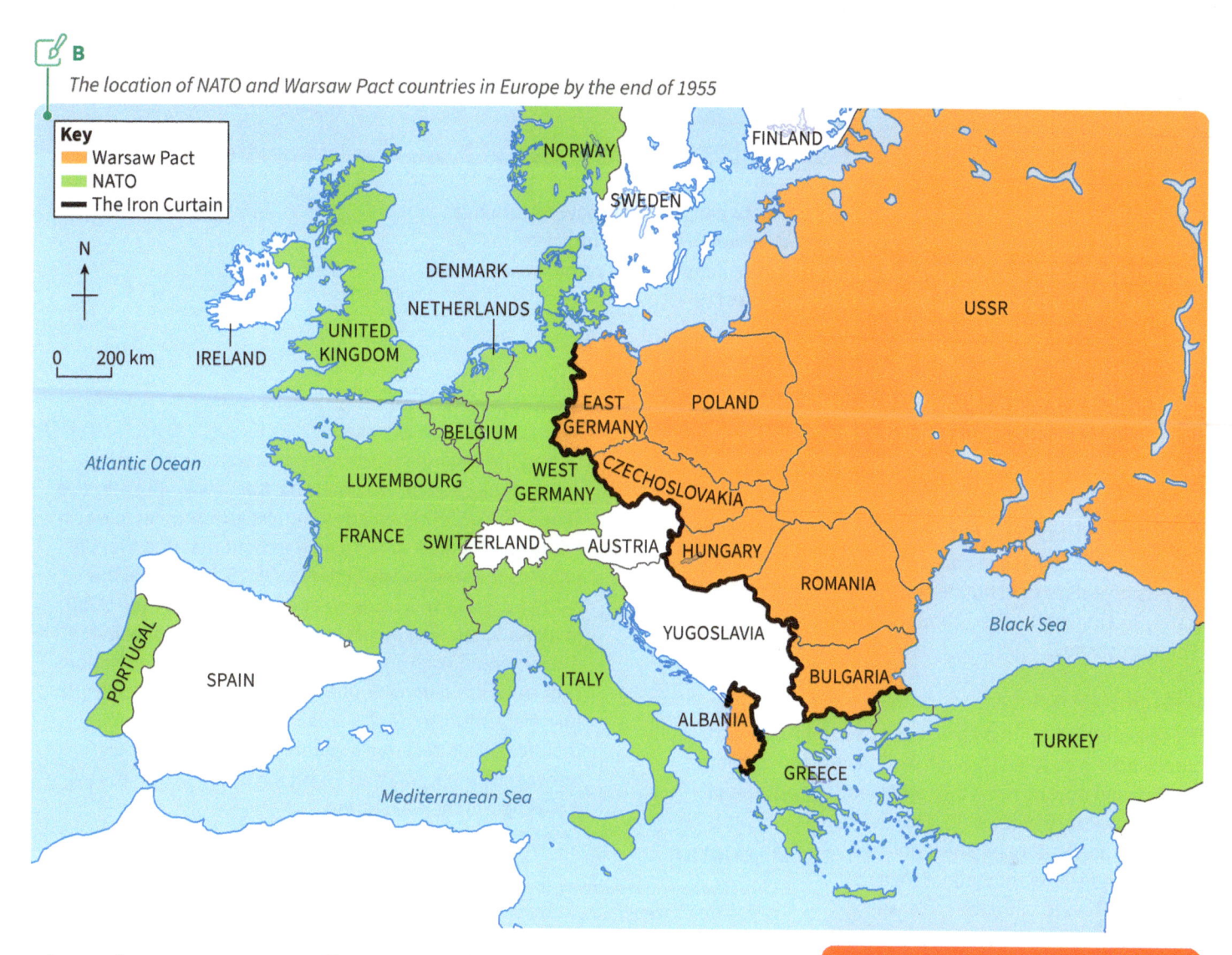

The main consequences of NATO and the Warsaw Pact

After nearly a decade of NATO and the Warsaw Pact, Europe was divided into two heavily armed alliances by the end of 1955. They had each promised their members to go to war to defend each other if necessary. This meant that only a small incident had the potential to push Europe fully into war.

However, some historians have argued that the two alliances made war less likely. Neither of the superpowers wanted to let their words or actions become an excuse for an all-out war, which would involve nuclear weapons and the threat of MAD.

Work

1. a. Create a quick fact-file for NATO. This could take the form of a table listing its key features, including who suggested it, why it was created and who its members were.
   b. Now do the same for the Warsaw Pact.
2. Look at **Source A**. Explain the message of the cartoon in your own words.
3. **Source A** gives a British perspective on NATO's formation. How surprising is it that it has a positive view of NATO? Explain your thinking.

Exam-style question

Write a narrative account analysing the key events between 1948 and 1955 that led to the creation of two opposing military alliances in Europe.

You **may** use the following:
- the Berlin blockade
- West Germany joining NATO

You **must** also use information of your own. (8 marks)

NAIL IT! Always check the dates you are given carefully. Often they are a useful clue about which events are most relevant. For narrative account questions in particular, they give you a hint about the event that started things off.

Chapter 3: The Cold War intensifies

3.3 How real was 'the thaw' after Stalin's death?

Objectives
- Identify who led the USSR after Stalin's death.
- Assess whether Stalin's death led to a thaw in relations.

After around eight years of worsening tensions between the superpowers, Stalin's death in 1953 gave leaders of the East and West an opportunity to improve their relations. But was the new leader, Nikita Khrushchev, really committed to 'thawing' the icy relationship between the two sides?

The death of Stalin

Stalin died of a stroke on 5 March 1953. Stalin's power had been so great that his death created a sense of insecurity; many people were unsure about what would happen next.

After a short power struggle between important Soviet politicians, Nikita Khrushchev emerged as the new leader of the USSR. He had been in charge of some of the most severe aspects of Stalin's rule, but he seemed more reasonable than Stalin, and at first the West thought it would be easier to work with Khrushchev.

Destalinisation

In February 1956, Khrushchev described Stalin as an extremely cruel leader who ruled through fear. He explained that the USSR would now be ruled differently and the process of 'destalinisation' would begin. This meant ending Stalin's harshest policies. Pictures and statues of Stalin were also removed. The secret police's role was reduced, but they were still active and monitored people for signs of disloyalty. There were also more consumer goods available.

Destalinisation was popular in the USSR. Western leaders hoped that relations would improve and that harsh Soviet rule over the satellite states would be relaxed. Khrushchev talked hopefully about 'peaceful coexistence' between East and West, where the two superpowers could leave each other and their separate spheres of influence alone. He said: 'We may argue. The main thing is to argue without using weapons.' A thaw in the icy relationship between the USA and the USSR seemed to be under way.

> **Meanwhile...**
>
> During the Second World War, Korea was controlled by Japan. When Japan was defeated, Korea was split into two zones. The USSR set up a communist government in North Korea and the USA set up a government that was friendly towards the West in South Korea. On 25 June 1950, the North Korean army, using weapons provided by the USSR, invaded South Korea, with the aim of creating one united – and communist – Korea. The USA and the United Nations sent troops to defend South Korea. China supported North Korea. Eventually the war ended, in 1953, in a stalemate (neither side is declared a winner). Today, the border between North Korea and South Korea is more or less as it was before the war started.

SOURCE A

Khrushchev (left) with US President Eisenhower (right) at the White House in 1959. After Stalin's death, the US and Soviet leaders met several times for talks.

Part 1: The origins of the Cold War 1941–58

Impact on the satellite states

Many people in the satellite states hoped that destalinisation would also improve their lives. Soon after Stalin's death, in June 1953, there was a revolt in East Germany over the strict rules that were making workers' lives very hard. However, this was brutally crushed by the communist authorities with support from the Red Army.

Loosening communist rule in the satellite states was difficult for Khrushchev to achieve without looking weak. If he allowed the Eastern bloc to become less reliant on the Soviets, it could have been the end of communism in Eastern Europe. This was because communist governments could be threatened by rebellions if people didn't think the Soviets would intervene. If this happened, Khrushchev would be removed from power by other Soviet leaders.

The creation of the Warsaw Pact in 1955 was a sign that the 'thaw' in relations was limited. The USSR clearly still felt threatened by NATO. Then in June 1956 there was a revolt in Poland against communist rule. Although it was again put down by the Red Army, Khrushchev did accept the Poles' choice of leader, Władysław Gomułka.

How real was the 'thaw' in US–Soviet relations?

There were promising signs of peaceful co-existence, such as destalinisation and meetings between the Soviet and US leaders. However, the arms race continued. Both sides had the more powerful H-bomb by the end of 1953, and continued to build their supplies of nuclear weapons throughout the 1950s. Both superpowers knew that the other side had enough nuclear weapons to destroy them several times over.

In the USA, fear of communism was at an all-time high. Known as the 'Red Scare', this was a period when some Americans falsely believed that there were communists in every aspect of US life. Senator Joseph McCarthy fuelled this scare, claiming that 57 members of the US government were Communist Party members. He also said that communists in the entertainment industry were putting out communist propaganda through books and films. McCarthy was found to be a fraud, but the public remained deeply concerned. Anyone hoping to be elected US president now had to promise to be tough on communism to stand a chance of winning.

SOURCE B

During the East German revolt against strict working conditions in 1953, this group of workers stood in front of the Brandenburg Gate in Berlin, burning flags showing the communist symbol.

Meanwhile…

Fear of communism in the West was known as the 'Red Scare' because communism was associated with the colour red. Communist propaganda used red to symbolise the blood of workers, shed in the struggle against capitalist oppression. This is why the army of the USSR was known as the 'Red Army'.

Exam-style question

Explain **two** consequences of Stalin's death for US–Soviet relations. (8 marks)

NAIL IT! The consequences you choose could refer to events, decisions or changes in attitudes. But, whatever you choose to explain, make sure you provide detail for each consequence: facts about what happened and facts about the impact of what happened.

Work

1. In your own words, describe what destalinisation was.
2. Compile a table with two columns: 'Evidence of a thaw' on one side, 'Evidence against a thaw' on the other side. Add examples for each.

3.4 'Seven days of freedom': the Hungarian Uprising, 1956

Objectives
- Identify key features of the dictatorship in Hungary before the uprising.
- Analyse the main reasons for the start of the uprising.
- Describe the reforms for Hungary planned by Imre Nagy.

Before dawn on 23 October 1956, a group of Hungarian students in Budapest, the capital, put up dozens of posters criticising the USSR. Their demonstrations later that day demanded free elections, a free press and the withdrawal of Soviet troops. They knew the USSR would respond angrily – but why did they hate communist rule so much to take this risk? How did Khrushchev respond? And how far did the popular new Hungarian Prime Minister Imre Nagy try to change Hungary?

Why did Hungarians hate Soviet rule?

During the Second World War, Hungary had been an ally of Nazi Germany. The Soviet Red Army invaded Hungary in September 1944, but in the November 1945 elections, the Communist Party won only 17 per cent of the vote. Even so, the Soviet representative in Hungary insisted on a **coalition government** – made up of the main political parties – with communists taking leading roles within it. In February 1947, some leaders of the non-communist parties were arrested, and many others fled Hungary.

Rákosi: the very strict communist leader

It was in these circumstances that Mátyás Rákosi became Hungary's new leader. He was strongly pro-Soviet, and set about imposing a dictatorship in Hungary, inspired by Stalin's methods (see table on page 43).

Demonstrations begin

Life in Hungary grew steadily harder after the Second World War. However, in 1956 some Hungarians saw reasons to be hopeful. Destalinisation was under way, and although the 1956 Polish revolt had been stopped, Khrushchev had agreed to some limited **reforms**. These reforms included allowing Gomułka, who was popular among Polish people, to remain as leader, and allowing the Polish government some limited independence from Soviet control.

The reforms in Poland inspired a number of Hungarian students, who began their demonstrations on 23 October 1956. As well as demanding free elections, a free press and the withdrawal of Soviet troops, the rebels pulled down a statue of Stalin and dragged it through the streets. AVO (Hungarian Secret Police) officers were violently attacked and many were killed. There were calls for Imre Nagy, a popular politician, to be made prime minister.

Khrushchev's response to the protests

The Soviet leader sent tanks to Budapest to deal with the protests the very next day, 24 October. They caused many casualties, but Khrushchev remained cautious. Very strict communism was clearly deeply unpopular, so he agreed later that day that Nagy could become prime minister to calm the situation.

SOURCE A
A Hungarian student describes the deep frustrations of living under Rákosi's regime

> Living standards were declining and yet the papers and radio kept saying that we had never had it so good. Why these lies? Everybody knew the state was spending the money on armaments. Why could they not admit that we were worse off because of this? I finally realised that the system was wrong and stupid.

Meanwhile...
In the mid-1950s, many African countries that had been colonies of European empires gained independence. Sometimes this process was peaceful. However, there were bloody and bitter struggles between the British and the Mau Mau of Kenya, and between the French and Algerians.

SOURCE B
A fifteen-year-old girl carrying a machine gun in Budapest during the Hungarian Uprising in 1956

Part 1: The origins of the Cold War 1941–58

Key words | coalition government | reforms | purge

Imre Nagy

- Imre Nagy (1896–1958) had been a committed communist since 1917.
- He became a leading politician in Hungary's communist government in the late 1940s.
- Nagy had a difficult relationship with Rákosi, because he believed Rákosi's policies were far too harsh.
- After the failure of the Hungarian Uprising, Nagy was arrested and sent to the USSR, where he was executed in 1958. Towards the end of the Cold War, Nagy's remains were reburied and 200,000 Hungarians paid tribute to him.

Nagy's reforms

Nagy managed to persuade the USSR to withdraw its troops on 28 October. The first stage of the Hungarian Uprising was over. However, what Nagy proposed next was very ambitious for a satellite state, and alarming to the USSR.

The following table compares the dictatorship set up in Hungary by Rákosi with the reforms proposed by Nagy in October 1956. The Soviets invaded Hungary before Nagy's reforms could be put into action.

Rákosi's Hungary	Nagy's reforms announced in October 1956
• 2000 Hungarians were killed in **purges** (when opponents of a government are rounded up and executed or imprisoned). • Hungary joined Comecon. It had to trade on unfair terms with the USSR. • Hungary also joined Cominform. Rákosi's government took orders from the Soviets. • Hungary's industry was strongly geared towards making weapons, not consumer goods, leading to a huge fall in living standards. There were often food shortages. • The Hungarian secret police (AVO) used terror to keep the population under control. • There was no freedom of speech or the press.	• Free elections. Other political parties would now be allowed. • Hungary would leave the Warsaw Pact and become a neutral country in the Cold War. • Freedom of speech and the press. • Hungary would start trading with the West.

Work

1. **a** Look at the table outlining features of Rákosi's Hungary. Divide them into political and economic features.
   b Now do the same for Nagy's reforms.
2. Draw a spider diagram outlining all the reasons why Hungarians hated communist rule.
3. Discuss with a partner which of Nagy's reforms you think might have angered the Soviets the most. Explain your reasons.

Exam-style question

Explain the following:

The importance of Soviet expansion in Eastern Europe for the Hungarian Uprising (1956). (8 marks)

NAIL IT! For this question, you need to think carefully about how the USSR setting up satellite states impacted upon Hungary specifically. Choose two main reasons why Hungarians revolted in 1956 and link these to Soviet aims in Eastern Europe at the end of the Second World War.

Chapter 3: The Cold War intensifies

3.5 How did Khrushchev and the world react to the Hungarian Uprising?

Objectives

- Explain Khrushchev's response to Nagy's reforms.
- Describe the Soviets' second invasion of Hungary in 1956.
- Assess the limited international response to the Soviet invasion.

Hungarians hoped that Nagy's reforms would free them from Soviet rule. However, just weeks after Nagy announced his plans, thousands of Hungarians – some of them children – lay dead after bitter fighting with invading Soviet troops. Why did Khrushchev decide to treat Hungary so brutally? And why did the West not come to the Hungarians' aid?

Khrushchev's response

For the Soviets, Nagy's reforms went too far. If Hungary left the Warsaw Pact, this would seriously threaten Soviet control over the satellite states, creating a gap in the Iron Curtain. Other Eastern bloc countries might soon follow. On 4 November 1956, 6000 Soviet tanks and 200,000 troops invaded Budapest.

SOURCE B

Soviet tanks in Budapest on 6 November 1956. Hungarians fought back, like this man on the tank, but they were no match for the strength of the invading Soviet force.

Hungarian resistance

In the days after 4 November, the Soviet army started to take control of Hungary. It was not easy: the Hungarians resisted, to defend their new freedoms. Some had guns, but they could not match the military equipment and training of the Soviets. Instead they used **guerrilla tactics**, such as setting ambushes for Soviet tanks in the streets. Teenagers and even children were involved.

It took two weeks in early November 1956 for the Soviets to crush the revolt. Between 3,000 and 20,000 Hungarians and around 700 Soviets were killed.

| Key word | guerrilla tactics |

SOURCE A
On 4 November 1956, Hungarian fighters broadcast a plea to the West via a station called Radio Free Europe

> There is no stopping the wild aggression of communism. Your turn will come, once we are killed. Save our souls! We beg you to help us in the name of justice and freedom.

Consequences of the Hungarian Uprising

Nagy had announced his ambitious reforms thinking that he could rely on support from the USA and the United Nations. But this support never came. Nagy was arrested and replaced by János Kádár, a hardline communist like Rákosi. Nagy was executed in 1958.

Kádár made sure Hungary was firmly back under Soviet control, reversing Nagy's reforms. The ruthless Soviet response to the revolt sent a clear warning to other satellite states not to move away from communism.

The international response

Sending Western military support to Hungary would have been extremely difficult, with Warsaw Pact countries ready to fight alongside the Soviets. The arms race also threatened to turn a dispute into a nuclear war. Moreover, most world leaders – and the UN – were distracted by the Suez Crisis in Egypt. Western aggression there made it seem hypocritical for the West to fight back against Soviet aggression in Hungary.

However, there was huge public sympathy for the Hungarians' suffering. There were demonstrations in Western Europe, and homes were offered to the 200,000 refugees who fled Hungary. $6 million was raised for them in an American charity appeal.

The uprising made it clear that the 'thaw' between the two superpowers had clear limits.

Meanwhile...
The Suez Canal is an artificial waterway that enables goods to be shipped between Europe and Asia without travelling around Africa. Since it was opened in 1869, it has been essential to international trade. In July 1956, Egyptian leader Abdul Nasser had taken control of the Suez Canal, which was owned and operated by Britain and France. Secretly, British and French leaders encouraged Israel to invade Egypt in October. Then they sent their own soldiers to take back control of the canal. This caused an international crisis. The USA even sided with the USSR when President Eisenhower strongly criticised Britain and France's aggression, and they were forced to withdraw.

Work

1. **a** Create a timeline of the key events in the Hungarian Uprising.
   b Highlight where the first and second phases of the uprising happened, and the two Soviet invasions.
2. Record the reasons why the West and the United Nations did not send military support to Hungary. In pairs, rank the reasons in order of importance.

Exam-style question
Explain **two** consequences of the Hungarian Uprising. (8 marks)

NAIL IT! It's important to choose two distinct consequences, which don't overlap. Here, you could write about one consequence for Hungary, and one consequence for superpower relations.

Chapter 3: The Cold War intensifies

Exam practice

How to... answer 'Explain two consequences...' questions

The 'Explain two consequences...' question is asking you to write about two things that happened as a result of an event.

Here is an example:

> **Exam-style question**
> Explain **two** consequences of the Yalta Conference. (8 marks)

Here is one way to answer this type of question.

1 Focus

- Identify the event in the question.

   The event in this question is the Yalta Conference, a major meeting that took place during the Second World War, in February 1945, between Churchill, Roosevelt and Stalin – the leaders of the most powerful Allied countries.

- Identify two things that happened as a result of the event. Remember, you are not being asked to write about the event itself or the causes of the event; you are being asked to write about what happened after it. And try to choose two very different consequences, perhaps one reaction from each side in the Cold War.

   Two consequences of the Yalta Conference were the division of Germany and the increase in Soviet control over Eastern Europe.

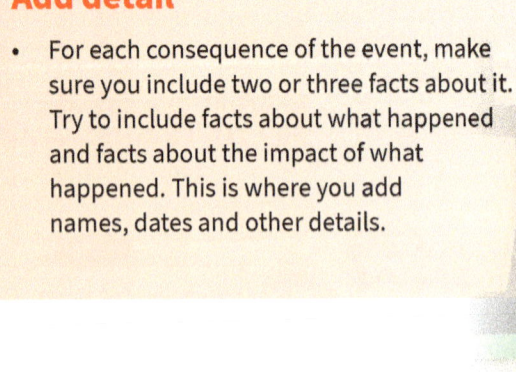

2 Add detail

- For each consequence of the event, make sure you include two or three facts about it. Try to include facts about what happened and facts about the impact of what happened. This is where you add names, dates and other details.

Part 1: The origins of the Cold War 1941–58

3 Write

- Answers to 'Explain two consequences...' questions *must* include regular use of language that shows the impact of an event. Use words and phrases like 'As a result of...', 'This led to...', 'This happened because...', 'which meant that...'.
- 'Explain two consequences...' questions are worth 8 marks and you should take about 10 minutes writing your answer. Top answers will contain two strong paragraphs, one for each consequence.

Study this sample paragraph. It's the first paragraph of an answer to the question we've been looking at.

Consequence 1
One consequence of the Yalta Conference was that Germany was divided into four separate zones. This happened because both the communist and the capitalist countries wanted to gain influence over defeated Germany after the Second World War. As a result of the division, the communist Soviets controlled East Germany, while the capitalist Allies controlled West Germany. West Berlin became an important capitalist area within the communist sphere, which meant that it became a significant reason for tension between the superpowers for many years, leading to events like the Berlin blockade (June 1948 to May 1949) and the building of the Berlin Wall (August 1961).

The first consequence the student has chosen to explain is neatly summarised in one sentence at the beginning of the paragraph.

Notice the use of language that shows what happened. It contains the phrases 'This happened because', 'As a result of' and 'which meant that.'

The paragraph contains lots of accurate detail. It includes facts about what happened (how Germany was divided after the Yalta Conference) and facts about the impact of what happened (the tension that resulted from the division).

This paragraph focuses throughout on one consequence of the Yalta Conference. In a full answer, the second paragraph should focus on a second consequence of the conference. For example, you could write about the fact that most countries in Europe – including Hungary, Czechoslovakia and Poland – would come under the Soviet sphere of influence after the end of the Second World War.

Work

1. Now have a go at completing the answer above by writing a second paragraph about a second consequence of the Yalta Conference.

2. Practise answering this question type by attempting the following question:

Exam-style question

Explain **two** consequences of the creation of NATO in 1949. (8 marks)

NAIL IT! Remember to support each consequence with specific facts about what happened, as well as facts about the impact of what happened.

Exam practice 47

4.1 Berlin: Khrushchev's ultimatum and the 1961 Vienna Summit

Objectives
- Describe the terms of Khrushchev's ultimatum over Berlin.
- Explain why West Berlin continued to embarrass the Soviets.
- Analyse the reasons for tension at the Vienna Summit.

In November 1958, Khruschev issued the Berlin ultimatum, demanding the West withdraw from West Berlin, but the West did not abandon the city. Instead the US and the USSR engaged in a series of summits to try to resolve the crisis. What led to the Berlin ultimatum? What happened at the summits? And why was the Vienna Summit of 1961 particularly disappointing for Khrushchev?

'A fishbone stuck in our throat'

Khrushchev used this phrase to describe the ongoing problems that West Berlin – and West Germany – posed for Soviet control over the Eastern bloc. West Germany was growing in economic and military strength in the early 1960s, and old Russian fears of a German invasion stayed strong.

The refugee crisis and the 'brain drain'

Many East Germans saw little future for themselves under communist rule and hoped to **defect** to West Germany. This meant that they wanted to leave communist rule for good and settle in the West. It was still fairly straightforward for East Germans to get to the West via West Berlin. Around 100,000 refugees from the communist bloc had crossed from East to West Germany this way between 1955 and 1960.

These numbers scared and embarrassed the Soviets and East Germans, but what made it worse was that many defectors were highly skilled and educated. Eastern bloc countries needed professional people such as scientists, mathematicians and engineers, so they had to stop this 'brain drain' to the West.

Khrushchev's Berlin ultimatum

In November 1958, Khrushchev gave the West a final demand – an ultimatum. He told the USA, Britain and France to withdraw their forces from West Berlin within six months and allow Berlin to become a neutral city instead. This started a new crisis over Berlin because the West refused to withdraw.

Superpower summits: 1959

Khrushchev and US President Eisenhower met twice in 1959 to try to resolve the tension over Berlin. They had a **summit** meeting in Geneva, Switzerland, in May. Although they could not agree on a solution, meeting face to face helped and they agreed to meet again at Camp David, a US residence for presidents, in September. Khrushchev agreeing to set foot on US soil was very significant and demonstrated good progress in relations. However, Berlin remained an unresolved issue and negotiations were set to continue in Paris in 1960.

Failure: the 1960 Paris Summit

Khrushchev's demand that the USA, Britain and France should withdraw their forces from West Berlin was dropped, but tension between the superpowers continued in other areas. This tension led to the total failure of the next summit in Paris.

On 1 May 1960, an American **U2** spy plane flying over Soviet territory was shot down by the USSR. At the Paris Summit two weeks later, President Eisenhower's refusal to apologise for the US plane being in Soviet airspace led Khrushchev to storm out of the meeting, leaving important issues including nuclear weapons and Berlin unresolved.

Key words | defect | summit | U2

SOURCE A

Soviets looking at the wreckage of the U2 spy plane, displayed in Moscow after it was shot down. The pilot was captured after crash landing and admitted to spying. The Soviets found spying equipment on the plane, although the USA denied it was a spy plane at first.

SOURCE C

A cartoon by Victor Weisz, published in the New Statesman, *a British magazine, on 14 May 1960*

Khrushchev vs Kennedy: the Vienna Summit in June 1961

At the next talks between the superpowers, held in Vienna, Austria, in June 1961, Khrushchev reissued the Berlin ultimatum. Several factors had boosted his confidence:

- John F. Kennedy had become President of the USA in January 1961; he was young and new to the job. Khrushchev was much more experienced.
- So far, the Soviets were winning the space race (see page 37). Three months earlier, the Russian Yuri Gagarin became the first human in space.
- Cuba, an island 165km from the US mainland, had recently become communist. Kennedy had been humiliated when a US-backed invasion of Cuba in 1961, aimed at removing its communist leader, Fidel Castro, ended in complete failure (see Chapter 5 for more about Cuba).

However, Kennedy stood his ground. He stuck to his promise of remaining tough on communism and rejected Khrushchev's ultimatum. Instead he increased the USA's spending on defence to $3.5 billion. With the question of Berlin completely unresolved, the Soviets and East Germany now took much bolder action to solve the refugee crisis.

SOURCE B

From Kennedy's first speech as US president, 20 January 1961. Here he is referring to the Soviet Union.

> Let every nation know, whether it wishes us well or ill, that we shall pay any price, bear any burden, meet any hardship, support any friend, oppose any foe, in order to assure the survival and the success of liberty.

Work

1. Make a brief timeline of the key events between 1958 and 1961 explored on these pages.

2. **a** Write a sentence or two to explain how each of these issues made Khrushchev feel more confident at the Vienna Summit in 1961:
   - the space race
   - the U2 incident
   - Cuba.

   b Now write a sentence or two explaining what Kennedy did at the Vienna Summit in 1961.

Exam-style question

Write a narrative account analysing the key events in US–Soviet relations between 1958 and 1961.

You **may** include the following in your answer:
- West Berlin
- the U2 incident

You **must** also use information of your own. (8 marks)

NAIL IT! Always read the question carefully. 'Key events' can include events that reduced tension as well as events that made relations worse.

Chapter 4: Flashpoint: Berlin

4.2 'Close the border!' The Berlin Wall

Objectives

- Describe the worsening of the refugee crisis in Germany.
- Examine how the Berlin Wall was constructed.
- Explain how the wall aimed to end defections to the West.

On 13 August 1961, Berliners woke to find a physical barrier being constructed, separating the western and eastern sides of the city. They could no longer cross the border between Western and Eastern Europe. It was now nearly impossible for East Germans to defect to the West, and many Berliners were separated from their jobs, families and friends. Why did the East German and Soviet authorities take such extreme action? What features did the Berlin Wall actually have? And what impact did it have upon the lives of Berliners?

The refugee crisis

Khrushchev had failed to convince the West to withdraw from West Berlin. The capitalist side of the city remained an embarrassment for the East and a worrying gap in the Iron Curtain. Defections had continued. The figures were alarming, and showed that the number of people leaving East Germany for the West was increasing very quickly:

- In June 1961, around 19,000 people left East Germany through Berlin.
- In July 1961, around 30,000 people left East Germany through Berlin.
- On 12 August 1961, about 2400 people crossed the border into West Berlin.

The defections gave Khrushchev a good reason for creating a hard physical barrier around West Berlin. Another reason was – Khrushchev argued – security. He claimed that West Berlin was a base for American spies, and that the communists needed to control and monitor access to the whole city.

Barbed wire and soldiers: the wall goes up

The East German leader, Walter Ulbricht, ordered the construction of a wall around West Berlin; Khrushchev did not stop him. Building began at 2:00am on 13 August 1961. At first, East German soldiers set up barbed wire barriers at the most frequently used crossing points on the East–West border, but soon the barrier stretched 43km encircling the whole of West Berlin. It was guarded by soldiers and dogs, and the East German authorities warned Berliners that anyone attempting to cross it would be shot.

Within days, most of the barbed wire fence was replaced by a concrete wall. This developed into a highly sophisticated and dangerous border (see diagram **A**).

A The Berlin Wall. By the 1980s, new features had been added to make it even harder to cross.

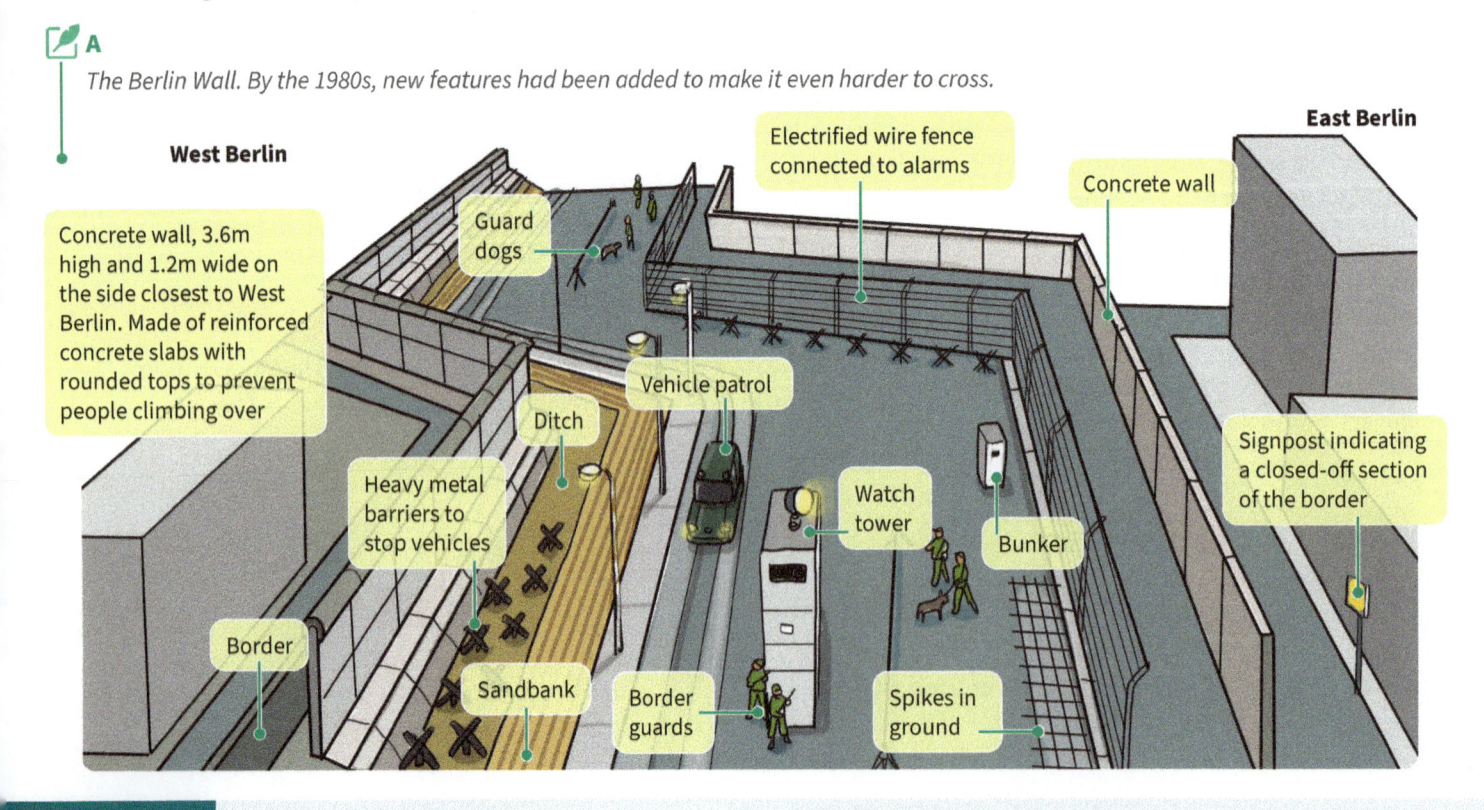

West Berlin | East Berlin

- Concrete wall, 3.6m high and 1.2m wide on the side closest to West Berlin. Made of reinforced concrete slabs with rounded tops to prevent people climbing over
- Guard dogs
- Electrified wire fence connected to alarms
- Concrete wall
- Ditch
- Vehicle patrol
- Watch tower
- Bunker
- Signpost indicating a closed-off section of the border
- Heavy metal barriers to stop vehicles
- Border
- Sandbank
- Border guards
- Spikes in ground

Part 2: Cold War crises 1958–70

The impact of the Berlin Wall on Germans

For many Berliners, the wall was a tragedy. Many families were now divided and wouldn't see each other until the wall came down in 1989. Those who had hoped to defect now had to accept living under communism. However, some still decided it was worth the risk and tried to escape. In the first year of the wall, 41 East Germans were shot while trying to cross it.

Ulbricht was more than satisfied with the Berlin Wall and believed it had resolved the refugee crisis, boosted the East German economy and weakened West Berlin.

SOURCE B

An extract from a letter Ulbricht wrote to Khrushchev in September 1961, describing the results of the wall so far

> We achieved the following things by closing the border around West Berlin:
>
> 1 The protection of East Germany against military provocation from West Berlin.
>
> 2 The end of the undermining of the East German economy by the West Berlin swamp.
>
> 3 …
>
> In West Berlin itself, the border areas are now empty. Many stores and cinemas are closed. West Berlin has finished playing its role as a show window of the capitalist West.

SOURCE C

An East German soldier patrols the Berlin Wall on 27 August 1961, while a crowd of West Berliners looks at the new barrier

Work

1. Make a table comparing the Berlin blockade of 1948–49 (see pages 32–35) with the Berlin Wall. These two events are very easily confused! Compare these features:
   - reasons for action
   - features
   - response (you will need to revisit this after you have studied the international response to the wall on the next page).

2. Use diagram **A** of the wall to explain in your own words why it was so hard for an East Berliner to cross to the West.

Exam-style question

Explain the following:

The importance of the failure of the summits between Khrushchev and American presidents (1959–1961) for the building of the Berlin Wall.

(8 marks)

NAIL IT! This question is asking you to explain one of the key reasons why the Berlin Wall was built: the failure of the superpowers to reach an agreement over West Berlin, despite attending several summits together. Think about how big a part Khrushchev's frustrations after each summit played in his decision to build the Berlin Wall.

Chapter 4: Flashpoint: Berlin

4.3
'Ich bin ein Berliner': the USA's reaction to the Berlin Wall

Objectives
- Describe the stand-off at Checkpoint Charlie in October 1961.
- Explain how the Berlin Wall reduced tensions between the superpowers.
- Analyse the Berlin Wall's status as a symbol of division in the Cold War.

For the East German authorities, the Berlin Wall was a success. However, West Berliners expected the USA to respond to the building of the wall. What did the USA do about the wall? How did the wall almost cause a war? And why did Kennedy say, 'I am a Berliner'?

The USA's reaction to the Berlin Wall

American officials were shocked by the news of the wall. Kennedy's first concern was the military security of West Berlin, so he sent Vice President Johnson and General Clay, the former US commander in West Berlin, there.

Nevertheless, Kennedy could see that the wall had ended the refugee crisis, and therefore decreased the tension over Berlin. He said to his colleagues, 'It's not a very nice solution, but a wall is a hell of a lot better than a war.'

October 1961: stand-off at Checkpoint Charlie

However, it didn't take long for the wall to create a dangerous situation between the USA and the USSR. Non-Germans could still pass between West and East Berlin, but the East German authorities checked their travel documents to ensure they had permission to do so. By making border crossing so difficult for the USA, the Soviets had broken a key agreement of the Yalta Conference in 1945.

SOURCE A

Checkpoint Charlie on 28 October 1961, when US tanks faced Soviet tanks in the stand-off

Part 2: Cold War crises 1958–70

The USA wanted to test how strict the communists would be about border crossings once the wall was up. On a few occasions, they sent troops and diplomats across the border peacefully, usually through **Checkpoint Charlie**. Then, in October 1961, the USA placed troops and tanks on the West Berlin side of the checkpoint. The East retaliated by placing its own troops on the other side. For several hours, the slightest incident between the two sides could have triggered a war.

However, neither side wanted this. Kennedy reassured Khrushchev that the West had no intention of using aggression and promised to withdraw the US troops near the wall if Khrushchev did the same. The stand-off was resolved.

Key word | Checkpoint Charlie

Kennedy in Berlin

Kennedy visited West Berlin in June 1963. By this point, the wall had become a famous symbol of the division of Europe, and of the huge divide between communism and capitalism. Around 1.5 million West Berliners (around two-thirds of its population) lined the streets to greet Kennedy. He then made a speech criticising the building of the wall and the communist system in general.

SOURCE B

Extracts from Kennedy's speech in West Berlin on 26 June 1963. It was directed at West Berliners, but Kennedy knew the Soviets were listening. 'Ich bin ein Berliner' is German for 'I am a Berliner'.

> There are many people in the world who really don't understand … what is the great issue between the free world and the Communist world. Let them come to Berlin.
>
> There are some who say that communism is the wave of the future. Let them come to Berlin.
>
> And there are some who say … we can work with the Communists. Let them come to Berlin.
>
> Freedom has many difficulties and democracy is not perfect. But we have never had to put a wall up to keep our people in. While the wall is the most obvious and vivid demonstration of the failures of the Communist system – for all the world to see – we take no satisfaction in it.
>
> Freedom is indivisible, and when one man is enslaved, all are not free … All free men, wherever they may live, are citizens of Berlin. And, therefore, as a free man, I take pride in the words: 'Ich bin ein Berliner.'

A propaganda victory for the West

Khrushchev was angry about Kennedy's words. Communist propaganda in the East described the wall as a necessary barrier against capitalist aggression. Most people were unconvinced, however, and saw the wall as a clear sign that the Soviet system was a failure.

The whole world knew about the wall, and one of the best-known incidents was the death of Peter Fechter, an 18-year-old East German who tried to cross the border on 17 August 1962. He was shot by East German guards and fell next to the wall, screaming for help. However, the East Germans did nothing, and the West Berliners could do nothing to help. Fechter took an hour to die.

Work

1. Using pages 50–53, create a mind-map exploring the different consequences of the Berlin Wall for Berliners, and for relations between the superpowers.

2. In pairs, analyse Kennedy's speech.
   a. What message was he trying to give to West Berliners?
   b. What message was he sending to the communists? If you can, watch a video online of him delivering the speech. Note the reaction of the crowd.

3. Create a table to help you keep the overview of events concerning Berlin between 1958 and 1961 clear in your head. Use these column headings: increasing tensions, crisis, resolution and impact.

Exam-style question

Explain **two** consequences of the building of the Berlin Wall. (8 marks)

NAIL IT! Make sure you add detail to develop your explanation of each consequence by including two or three facts about it. Include names, dates and other details.

Chapter 4: Flashpoint: Berlin

5.1 America's backyard: revolution in Cuba

Objectives
- Describe the events of the Cuban Revolution.
- Explore how life changed in Cuba.

For most Americans in the 1950s, the Cold War was something that was happening far away in Europe and had little direct impact on their lives. On 1 January 1959, this changed dramatically when Fidel Castro led a revolution in Cuba – a country just 165km from the US coast. Communism was now in America's backyard. Why did Castro become popular in Cuba? What changes did he bring to the country? Why did Cuba become allied with the USSR?

Batista's Cuba

Before the revolution, Cuba was under the control of one man: Fulgencio Batista. Batista's corrupt government made huge amounts of money doing deals with American businesspeople. The government was undemocratic and any opposition was dealt with quickly and often brutally. Despite this, in the early 1950s increasing numbers of Cubans began to challenge the government, and a young lawyer named Fidel Castro called for revolution. He was forced to leave Cuba in 1953 but he and his growing number of supporters immediately began to plan for their return.

Castro's revolution

In 1956, Castro and 81 supporters, including his younger brother Raul and an Argentinian revolutionary called Che Guevara, returned to Cuba. The group, who became known as Los Barbudos (the bearded ones), began a two-year **guerrilla war** in which they attacked important government sites and built support among the Cuban people. Slowly, Batista's grip on power weakened and on 1 January 1959 his government collapsed and he fled the country. The following day, Castro entered the capital, Havana, and took power.

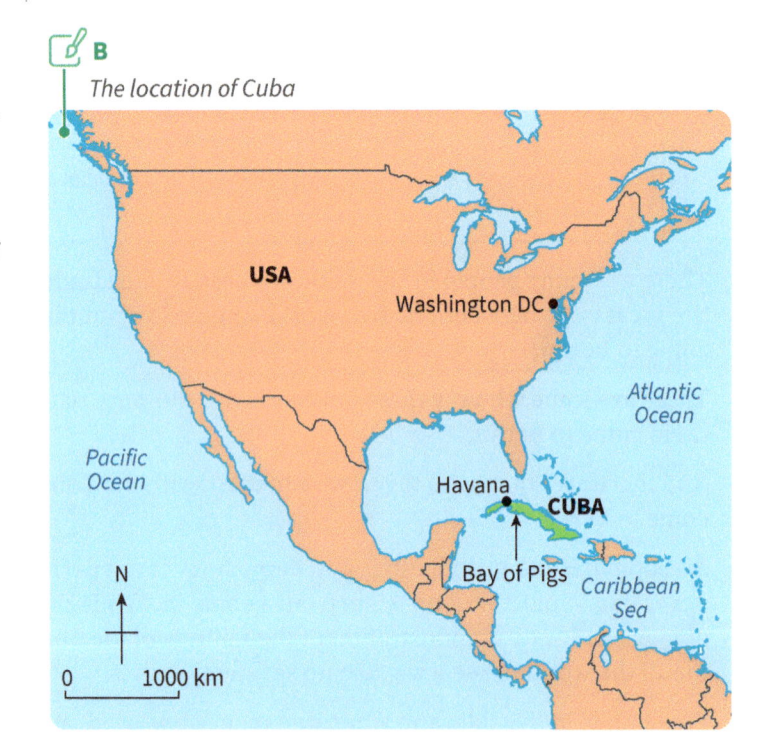

B
The location of Cuba

SOURCE A
A US government report on Batista's Cuba, written by the American historian and political commentator Arthur Schlesinger during the 1950s

> The corruption of the Government, the brutality of the police, the regime's indifference to the needs of the people for education, medical care, housing, for social justice and economic justice is an open invitation to revolution.

SOURCE C
A painting to commemorate the Cuban Revolution. The text says 'Havana January 1 1959: Batista flees'.

Key words | guerrilla war | embargo

Cuba and the superpowers

Before the revolution, Castro had not talked about communism explicitly. However, he was clearly a firm believer in left-wing ideas. He said he wanted to take control of the country for the people of Cuba and his government took over many of Cuba's industries, and made changes to the way the ownership of farmland was organised. This involved taking control of many businesses and farms owned by Americans in Cuba. In April 1959, he visited the USA, keen to show that he wanted to work with Cuba's powerful neighbour. President Eisenhower, concerned about what was happening, refused to meet him.

As the USA was unwilling to work with him, Castro turned to an obvious alternative – the other superpower, the Soviet Union. The USSR was willing to provide loans and oil to Cuba. In response, in 1961, the USA declared an **embargo** on the country – banning any business or trade between Cuba and the USA. Cuba was now firmly aligned with and reliant on the USSR.

Fidel Castro (1927–2016)

- The son of a wealthy farmer, Castro became interested in politics – and the idea of revolution – while studying to be a lawyer.
- In 1953, he was forced to leave Cuba and spend time in Mexico. He returned in 1956 to lead the revolution against Batista. After the revolution, he became leader of Cuba.
- He then reorganised Cuba into a communist-style one-party state, with all aspects of life tightly controlled, including the media and free speech. Opponents faced torture or execution.
- His government introduced health care for all citizens, hugely improving this aspect of many people's lives.
- Despite numerous attempts by the USA to remove him from power, Castro remained Cuba's dictator until 2008, when he retired and power transferred to his younger brother Raul.

Later on…

Ernesto 'Che' Guevara (1928–67) was a key figure in Castro's revolution. He was also involved in several other revolutionary movements in South America. From the 1960s onwards, he became a symbol of revolution and challenge to authority. His image is very famous and can be seen on T-shirts, posters and other products all over the world!

Exam-style question

Write a narrative account analysing the key events of the Cuban Revolution (1956–59).

You **may** use the following in your answer:
- Batista
- Cuba's alliance with the USSR

You **must** also use information of your own. (8 marks)

NAIL IT! For a narrative question you need to consider the three parts of the story: beginning, middle and end. For this question, this is likely to be Cuba under Batista, Castro taking power, and the consequences for relations with the superpowers.

Work

1. **a** Who was in charge of Cuba before the revolution in 1959?
   b According to **Source A**, what was life like in Cuba before the revolution in 1959?

2. Why were many Cubans keen to support Castro?

3. Create a three-part flow diagram that tells the story of the Cuban Revolution. Use the following titles to help you:
   - causes
   - events
   - consequences.

4. Why did Cuba become allied with the USSR? Explain your answer using specific facts.

Chapter 5: Flashpoint: Cuba   55

5.2 What happened at the Bay of Pigs?

Objectives
- Outline the plan and the events of the 'Bay of Pigs' invasion.
- Examine the reasons for the outcome.
- Assess the impact on superpower relations.

By 1961, with a communist country so close to the American coast, new US President Kennedy felt that he had to take action. Keen not to provoke the USSR with a full-scale invasion of Cuba, he came up with a more secretive plan. He set out to help Cubans who were against Castro, and who had fled to Florida in the south of the USA, to invade and take control of the country. How exactly would the plan work? How successful was it? What were the consequences of the invasion?

Why was Kennedy so worried?

Although most Americans did not see Cuba as a direct threat, the domino theory warned them that now that Cuba had fallen to communism, other countries in the area might do the same. There was growing support for communism across South and Central America and so this threat seemed very real, and very urgent. Kennedy believed that removing Castro would stop other revolutions from taking place in these areas.

The plan

After Castro's victory with the Cuban revolution, many supporters of the former leader, Batista, had fled Cuba and settled in the USA. This large group of **exiles** were key to the American plan. They would be trained by the US intelligence agency – the **CIA** – to invade Cuba at the Bay of Pigs, around 70km from the capital, Havana. The US air force would support the exiles by attacking Cuban defences. It was thought that the invasion would inspire other Cubans to join the fight and overthrow Castro and his government.

The invasion

Just before the invasion was launched, Kennedy changed his mind about involving the US air force. He was concerned that US involvement would go against international law because it is generally viewed as unacceptable to remove another country's leader. The invasion at the Bay of Pigs was launched on 17 April 1961 but without US planes: this meant the exiles were left totally exposed, and were easily defeated and captured. It was also made clear that most Cubans were now loyal to Castro and were not willing to fight alongside the exiles. Castro had won a great victory against his much more powerful neighbour, and Kennedy and the USA were left feeling embarrassed.

Meanwhile...

As the superpowers fought for influence in Cuba, there were similar situations happening in parts of Africa. As old European empires broke up, and more and more African countries became independent, the USA and the USSR worked – often ruthlessly – to bring these countries onto their side in the Cold War. Guinea was one key example: in 1958, Soviet support made the government loyal to the USSR, but by 1961, a huge effort by Kennedy meant that Guinea was now in the American camp.

Part 2: Cold War crises 1958–70

Key words   exile | CIA

The consequences

Despite the lack of American planes, US involvement was obvious. Kennedy's political opponents said he was too young and inexperienced to handle such important matters, and they seemed to have been proved right. Even more concerning for Kennedy was that the event had made him look weak. This was not a good position to be in as he headed into his first meeting with Soviet leader Khrushchev in June 1961.

For Castro, the victory was cause for celebration. However, he was aware that the USA would not give up and that he remained vulnerable. The incident pushed Cuba into an even closer alliance with the USSR, and contributed towards increased tension between the superpowers in the following year.

SOURCE A

Captured Cuban exiles after the failed Bay of Pigs invasion, April 1961

SOURCE B

From a speech made by Castro in 1962. 'Yankee' is a nickname for Americans.

What is hidden behind the Yankee's hatred of the Cuban Revolution? A small country of only seven million people, economically underdeveloped, without financial or military means to threaten the security or economy of any other country? What explains it is fear. Not fear of the Cuban Revolution but fear of the Latin [South and Central] American Revolution.

Work

1. Why was Kennedy so concerned about the Cuban Revolution?

2. Look at **Source B**. Does this support your answer to question 1? Include a quote from the source in your answer.

3. Create a storyboard of the Bay of Pigs invasion. You should include:
   - the plan
   - the last minute changes
   - the invasion itself
   - the failure of the invasion
   - the consequences for Kennedy and Castro.

Exam-style question

Explain **two** consequences of the Bay of Pigs invasion (1961).

(8 marks)

NAIL IT! If you are struggling to think of consequences for this question type, think about the impact of the event on superpower relations. Did the event improve them, or create more tension? The Bay of Pigs clearly created more tension because it pushed Castro into a closer alliance with the USSR.

Chapter 5: Flashpoint: Cuba   57

5.3A
The Cuban Missile Crisis

Objectives
- Describe the events of the Cuban Missile Crisis.
- Explain how the events developed and escalated.

Since the early 1950s, the USA had located nuclear weapons in various places in Europe. Some were in Turkey, and if launched from there, they could easily reach and destroy Moscow and other Soviet cities. The USSR, however, could not place weapons close enough to attack the USA. The USSR's alliance with Cuba offered the chance to change this, and in the summer of 1962, Khrushchev ordered Soviet nuclear missiles to be installed there, just 165km from the American coast. What were the consequences of this decision? How did the USA respond? How close did the world really come to total nuclear destruction?

Missiles in Cuba

Following the failed Bay of Pigs invasion, Cuba's alliance with the USSR had become even closer. Castro knew that he was vulnerable to another attack from the USA and so needed the support of another powerful country. For the Soviet leader, Nikita Khrushchev, having an ally so close to the USA was an opportunity to be seized. It was the perfect place to base Soviet missiles, with US cities including Washington DC, New York and Los Angeles well within their range. The USA had missiles in Turkey, which could be used to attack Soviet cities, so it was also the chance to match the American position.

The first Soviet missiles were transported to Cuba in the summer of 1962, but it took until 14 October for the Americans to realise what was happening when a U2 spy plane photographed a number of missile sites on the island. President Kennedy's reaction would be key to what happened next.

The American response

Kennedy took some time to consider his response, spending a week with his key advisers, a committee known as **ExComm**. On 21 October he introduced a **quarantine** on Cuba, stopping all ships from reaching the island with a blockade created by US navy ships. On 22 October, he addressed the American people and explained the situation: DEFCON 3, the third highest state of security alert. Kennedy told his brother Robert that he had taken 'one hell of a gamble'. He knew that he had drawn a clear line, and if the Soviets crossed it, there would be war.

SOURCE A

An aerial photograph of a missile site, taken by an American U2 spy plane. It shows that Soviet missile sites had been built in Cuba.

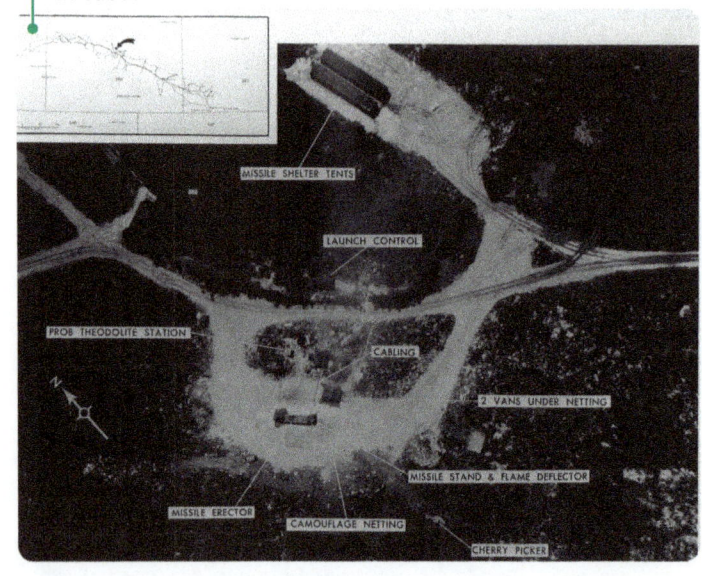

B

The distances that short- and long-range nuclear missiles could reach from Cuba

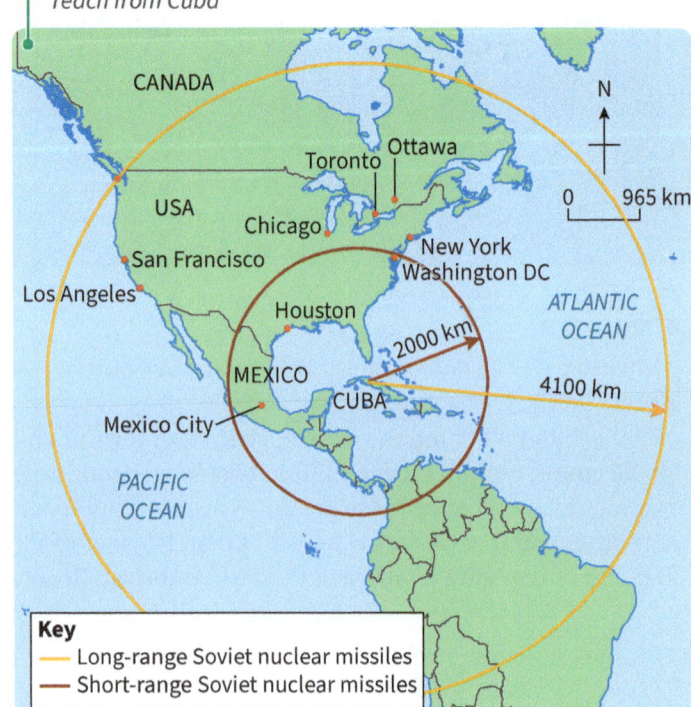

58 Part 2: Cold War crises 1958–70

Key words | quarantine | ExComm | Secretary-General | brinkmanship

C
The DEFCON system

DEFCON 1:	Nuclear war is imminent or has already started
DEFCON 2:	Next step is nuclear war; armed forces ready to deploy and engage in less than six hours
DEFCON 3:	Increased readiness; air force ready to launch in 15 minutes
DEFCON 4:	Increased alert and strengthened security measures
DEFCON 5:	Lowest state of alert

The Soviet response

Khrushchev was concerned the USA would see the missiles as an excuse to invade Cuba and wanted to be ready. On 23 October, a group of Soviet ships approached Cuba, carrying more missiles. The **Secretary-General** of the United Nations called for calm, and on 24 October, Khrushchev ordered his ships to stop. There was now a stand-off in the Atlantic. With the USA moving to DEFCON 2, movement from either side could lead to war. This was now a game of **brinkmanship** – pushing your opponent right to the limit – with unimaginable consequences.

Meanwhile…
The DEFCON system was created in 1959 to describe the level of alert of the US military forces. It was used throughout the Cold War. DEFCON 2 has only been reached twice – during the Cuban Missile Crisis and at the start of the Gulf War in the Middle East in 1991.

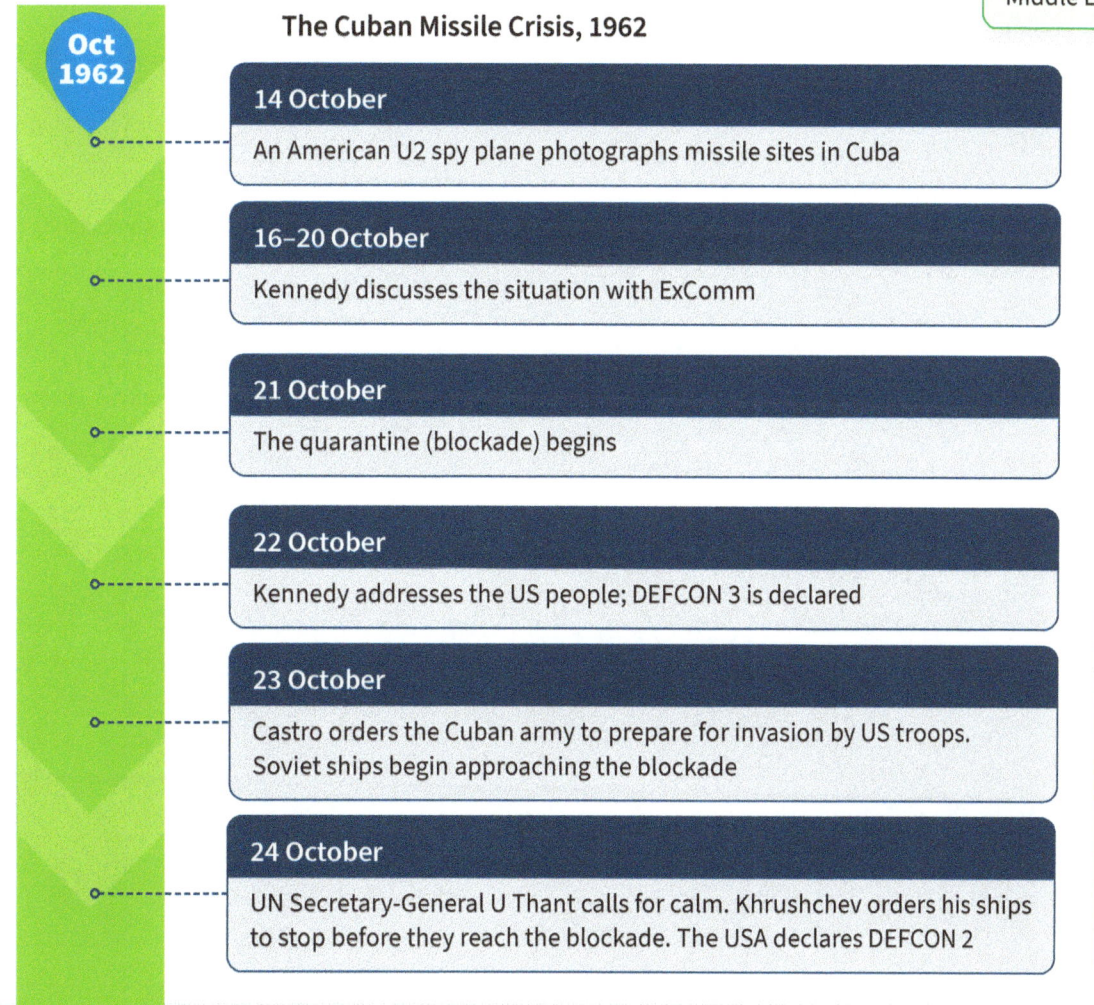

The Cuban Missile Crisis, 1962

Oct 1962

14 October
An American U2 spy plane photographs missile sites in Cuba

16–20 October
Kennedy discusses the situation with ExComm

21 October
The quarantine (blockade) begins

22 October
Kennedy addresses the US people; DEFCON 3 is declared

23 October
Castro orders the Cuban army to prepare for invasion by US troops. Soviet ships begin approaching the blockade

24 October
UN Secretary-General U Thant calls for calm. Khrushchev orders his ships to stop before they reach the blockade. The USA declares DEFCON 2

Work
1. Why was the USA so concerned by the presence of missiles in Cuba?
2. How far do you think Kennedy's response made the situation worse?

Chapter 5: Flashpoint: Cuba 59

5.3B

With Soviet and American ships facing each other in the Atlantic, and both sides on a high level of alert, nuclear war seemed not just possible, but likely. As the world looked on, the events of the Cuban Missile Crisis continued to unfold. Which side would back down first? Would either be willing to risk nuclear war?

A world on the brink

At 7:15am on Thursday 25 October 1962, a Soviet ship entered the US quarantine zone. It was stopped by the US navy but was then allowed to pass. As the ship had been an oil tanker it was not seen as a threat, but it was clear that Khrushchev was seeking to provoke Kennedy.

The following day, on 26 October, preparations began in the USA for a possible invasion of Cuba – 12,000 troops were assembled in Florida, awaiting orders. Kennedy was reluctant but ready. Later that day, with tensions high, a telegram arrived from Khrushchev. It promised that the USSR would remove the missiles from Cuba, if Kennedy promised not to invade Cuba. Khrushchev, it seemed, had been the one to back down. The crisis, however, was not yet over.

A Soviet sub and two American planes

Just as things seemed to be calming down, on 27 October an American battleship detected a Soviet B-59 submarine close to Cuba. The US ship began attacking the submarine with depth charges (bombs that send shockwaves through the water), trying to bring it to the surface. It later became clear that the submarine, which had nuclear missiles called **torpedoes** on board, was totally out of contact with the rest of the Soviet navy. The captain, believing war had begun, gave the command to launch a torpedo. Luckily a more senior officer happened to be on board and overruled the captain.

That same morning, the Cubans shot down a US spy plane. The order had been given by a low-ranking officer, who had not checked with his commander. Later in the day, another US plane drifted into Soviet airspace near the American state of Alaska. The Soviets fired on the plane, but it escaped. Any of these events, all beyond the direct control of Kennedy or Khrushchev, could have led to war. Both governments now recognised how dangerous a game they were playing.

SOURCE A

The wreckage of the U2 spy plane shot down over Cuba on 27 October. The pilot, Major Rudolf Anderson, was the only person killed during the Cuban Missile Crisis.

| Key word | torpedo |

Disaster averted

Before the Americans had responded to Khrushchev's first telegram, a second one arrived. Once again Khrushchev said that he would remove the missiles from Cuba – but this time he demanded that US missiles should be withdrawn from Turkey. Kennedy did not want to be seen to be giving in, but as the alternative was nuclear war, he had no choice but to accept. There was one condition – the missile removal from Turkey was to be kept secret. As far as the public was concerned, it was Khrushchev's first telegram to which Kennedy was responding.

Kennedy announced the end of the blockade. Both sides rushed to claim victory – Kennedy claimed to have forced Khrushchev to back down, while Khrushchev claimed to have acted in the interest of world peace to end the crisis. The brinkmanship was over, and the world had survived!

SOURCE B

A British cartoon by Leslie Gilbert Illingworth, published in the Daily Mail *in 1962*

Oct 1962

25 October
A Soviet tanker crosses the US blockade but is allowed to pass

26 October
US troops prepare to invade Cuba. Khrushchev sends his first telegram to Kennedy

27 October
A Soviet submarine is detected off the coast of Cuba; a US plane is shot down over Cuba while another drifts into Soviet airspace near Alaska

Khrushchev sends his second telegram. Kennedy agrees to secretly remove the US missiles from Turkey in exchange for Soviet missiles leaving Cuba. The blockade is lifted and the crisis is over

Work

1. a What was the key development on 25 October?
   b Why was this such a moment of tension?

2. Create an illustrated flow diagram to show how the events of the Cuban Missile Crisis developed. Think about a clear beginning, a middle and an end, and create one box in the flow diagram for each.

3. a Why do you think Kennedy accepted the demands in Khrushchev's second telegram?
   b Do you think he had a choice? Explain your answer.

4. Look at **Source B**.
   a Describe what you can see in this source.
   b What point is it making about the Cuban Missile Crisis?

Exam-style question

Write a narrative account analysing the key events of the Cuban Missile Crisis (1962).

You **may** use the following in your answer:
- the blockade
- Khrushchev's second telegram

You **must** also use information of your own. (8 marks)

NAIL IT! Think about your answer as if it is a story; it needs a beginning, a middle and an end. What is the beginning, middle and end of the story of the Cuban Missile Crisis?

Chapter 5: Flashpoint: Cuba

5.4 The consequences of the Cuban Missile Crisis

Objectives
- Summarise the consequences of the Cuban Missile Crisis.
- Examine the short- and longer-term consequences.
- Assess the state of superpower relations in the 1960s.

The Cuban Missile Crisis of 1962 was arguably the closest that the superpowers came to nuclear war. With destruction avoided, Kennedy and Khrushchev began to think about how to avoid a similar event happening again. For both leaders, the crisis was the biggest test of their leadership, and it was clear that relations between the superpowers may need a different approach in future.

The consequences for Khrushchev and the USSR

Khrushchev claimed he had removed the missiles from Cuba to promote world peace, and suggested that the USSR's actions during the crisis had been to help a small country stand up to the bullying of the USA. Cuba remained an ally of the USSR and a constant embarrassment to the USA. Unfortunately for Khrushchev, his greatest success out of the crisis – the removal of US missiles from Turkey – was kept a secret from the world, and he could not claim any public credit. Many senior figures in the USSR felt that Khrushchev had been reckless throughout the crisis, while others thought he had given in too easily. Most agreed that he had not handled it well. Although there were other factors, there is no doubt that Khrushchev's handling of the Cuban Missile Crisis was one of the reasons for his removal from power two years later.

Kennedy and the USA

After the embarrassment of the Bay of Pigs, Kennedy had shown the world that he could make difficult decisions and be a tough negotiator. This silenced many of his critics. The removal of missiles from Cuba meant that there was no longer a direct nuclear threat to the USA. To the public, this seemed to have been achieved without having to give anything up in return. In reality, the removal of missiles from Turkey was a huge compromise. As long as this stayed secret, however, President Kennedy looked strong and would remain popular.

SOURCE A
The front page of an American newspaper from 29 October 1962

New York Mirror
K BOWS! Will Pull Out Missiles
Kennedy Made No Deals

SOURCE B
From the autobiography of Fidel Castro, published in 2008. He is describing his reaction to the end of the crisis. The 'conditions' that Castro is referring to are the conditions in the agreement reached between the superpowers which ended the Cuban Missile Crisis, including the removal of all nuclear weapons from Cuba.

> We weren't opposed to the solution, because it was important to avoid a nuclear conflict. But Khrushchev should have told the Americans, 'The Cubans must be included in the discussions.' … out of principle, they should have consulted with us. Had they done that, the conditions would most certainly have been better.

Key word	hotline

Was the world a safer place after the crisis?

The Cuban Missile Crisis drew attention to how quickly the leaders of the two superpowers could lose control of events. It took the two leaders communicating directly with each other to remove any misunderstandings and end the crisis. In order to avoid a possible misunderstanding in the future, a direct line of contact known as the '**hotline**' was created so that, in times of high tension, the two leaders could always speak directly to each other.

Kennedy and Khrushchev also recognised that continuously building more powerful nuclear weapons was making the world an ever more dangerous place. In 1963, they passed the Limited Test Ban Treaty, which banned the testing of nuclear weapons above ground. Then, in 1968, the two superpowers, along with the UK, signed the Nuclear Non-proliferation Treaty, which aimed to stop the spread of nuclear weapons to other countries. Despite these treaties both the USA and the USSR continued to hold huge stockpiles of nuclear weapons.

SOURCE C

A cartoon by the American cartoonist Herblock in November 1962

"LET'S GET A LOCK FOR THIS THING"
NUCLEAR WAR
HERBLOCK

Meanwhile…

While the Cuban Missile Crisis and its aftermath unfolded, other areas of the world saw important developments in the Cold War.
- Across South America, groups inspired by the success in Cuba started guerrilla warfare campaigns to try to bring communism to their countries. The USA became increasingly involved in funding anti-communists. In 1964, military forces in Brazil overthrew a government that was believed to have communist connections. It is widely accepted that the US intelligence agency, the CIA, was involved.
- By 1963, Vietnam was divided in two. North Vietnam was under communist control, while South Vietnam was allied to the USA. The USA's determination to stop any further spread of communism would see the Americans drawn into a lengthy and brutal war in Vietnam.

Later on…

After the Cuban Missile Crisis, Cuba remained an ally of the USSR and supported communism around the world, often sending troops to support communist fighters in South America, Africa and the Middle East. With the US ban on trade still in place, Cuba relied on the USSR for financial support. Despite this coming to an end in 1991, when the Soviet Union collapsed, Castro's communist government continues to hold power. Castro retired as leader in 2011 and was replaced by his younger brother, Raul, who ruled until 2021. Recently, relations between the USA and Cuba have improved, but tensions remain.

Work

1. a Make a list of the ways in which the Cuban Missile Crisis could be seen as both a victory and a defeat for Khrushchev.
    b Now do the same for Kennedy.
    c Which leader do you think has the best claim to victory?

2. Read **Source B**.
    a How does Castro feel about the deal that was done to end the crisis?
    b 'Cuba was a witness, rather than a player in the Cuban Missile Crisis.' How far do you agree? Explain your answer.

3. Look at **Source C**.
    a What does this cartoon suggest will be the consequence of the crisis?
    b How far was this the case?

Exam-style question

Explain the following:

The importance of the Cuban Missile Crisis (1962) for superpower relations.

(8 marks)

NAIL IT! When considering the importance of an event, think about the importance in the short term and the importance in the long term. In the case of the Cuban Missile Crisis, you could think about its immediate impact on superpower relations and the ways in which it led to greater cooperation in the long term.

Chapter 5: Flashpoint: Cuba 63

6.1A
The Prague Spring

Objectives
- Describe the key developments of the Prague Spring and the changes that were introduced.
- Explain the Soviet response.
- Evaluate the consequences of the Prague Spring.

By the 1960s, the difference in people's lives either side of the Iron Curtain had become more obvious. While Western Europeans enjoyed new technologies and products, in the East life was harder. People had limited freedom and limited access to basic goods, and the luxuries that were enjoyed in the West were scarce. In Czechoslovakia, a new leader, Alexander Dubček, responded to the growing anger and sense of unfairness in the country by attempting to bring about change. His reforms, known as the Prague Spring, would be the biggest challenge to Soviet control since the Hungarian Uprising of 1956. What was life like in Czechoslovakia before the Prague Spring? How did life change after Dubček's reforms? And how did the Soviets respond?

Life before the Prague Spring

Like all the countries behind the Iron Curtain, Czechoslovakia was tightly controlled by the Communist Party. Although it had its own government, it was entirely answerable to the Soviet government in Moscow. No opposition was allowed, and the media was heavily restricted. People's lives were hard and the clear corruption (including the taking of bribes) of the country's leader, Antonín Novotný, and other officials added to the sense of anger and unfairness in the early to mid-1960s.

In the mid-1960s, an economist named Ota Šik called for reforms, including allowing private business to exist and giving some political power to the people. He also said that the government should be more ready to listen to people's concerns. The USSR rejected all of his ideas, but other Czechoslovakians were inspired by them. It was clear that something needed to be done to avoid a revolt and, in January 1968, Moscow forced Novotný to resign.

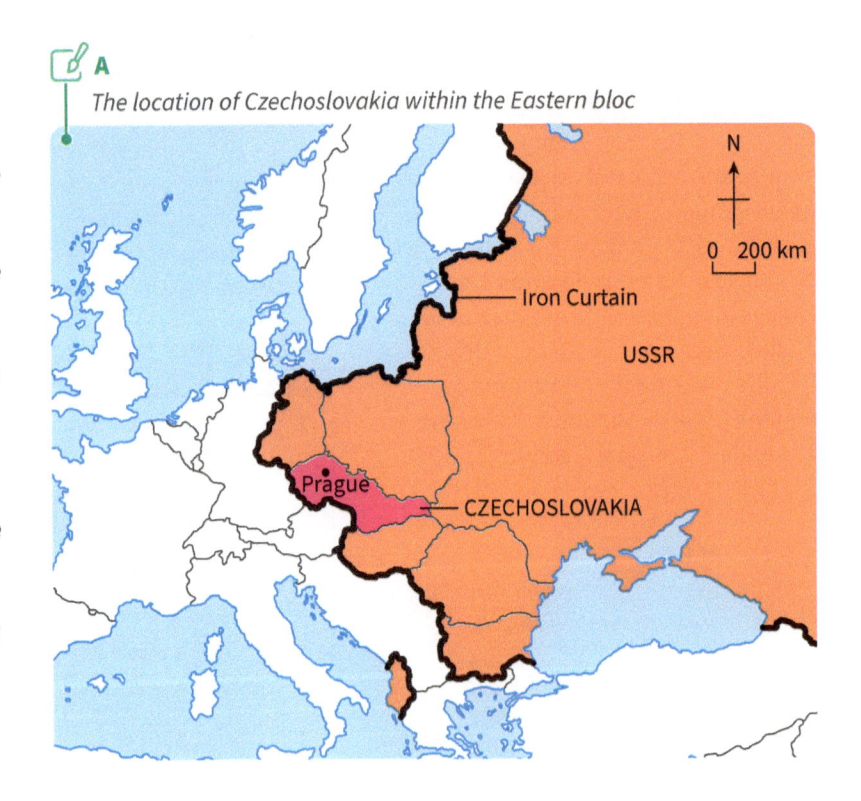

A
The location of Czechoslovakia within the Eastern bloc

Dubček's reforms

Novotný was replaced in 1968 by another senior communist, Alexander Dubček. The Soviets believed that he would calm the situation but instead he began introducing many of the reforms that people were calling for. He declared '**socialism** with a human face' – in other words, the country would continue to work towards being communist, but would treat its citizens with more compassion.

Dubček's reforms included:
- allowing Czechoslovakians to run their own businesses
- allowing freedom of speech and public meetings
- stopping censorship of the press
- allowing Czechoslovakians to visit non-communist countries
- allowing trade unions and other political groups to form (although the Communist Party would remain the only one in government).

64   Part 2: Cold War crises 1958–70

Key word: socialism

Dubček said that both he and Czechoslovakia were still loyal to the Communist Party and the Warsaw Pact, but Moscow was unhappy with his changes, fearing a loss of control. The USSR did not stop the reforms, however, and Dubček pressed on with even more. The changes became known as the Prague Spring, after Czechoslovakia's capital city. The world now watched and waited for the Soviet government to respond.

SOURCE B

Adapted from Hope Dies Last, *the autobiography of Alexander Dubček, published in 1993*

> [The reforms were] immediately viewed by the Soviets as the beginning of a return to capitalism. Brezhnev [the new Soviet leader] made this accusation directly during one of our conversations in the coming months. I responded that we needed thriving shops and businesses that produced lots of goods so that people's lives would be easier. Brezhnev immediately snapped at me, 'Small craftsmen? We know about that!' Here was the old communist idea of small businesses leading to capitalism. There was nothing I could do to change the Soviets' paranoia.

Alexander Dubček (1921–92)

- Born in Czechoslovakia but spent most of his childhood in the Soviet Union. He returned to his home country during the Second World War to join the fight against the Nazis.
- After the war he rose through the ranks of the Communist Party and became Czechoslovakia's leader in 1968.
- He was forced from power in 1969 and expelled from the Communist Party the following year.
- After the collapse of the USSR, he returned to politics in 1989 and was seen as a national hero.
- He was killed in a car crash in 1992.

Work

1. What was life like in Czechoslovakia before 1968?
2. In your own words, explain the changes that Dubček made when he became leader.
3. Read **Source B**.
   a. According to the source, what concerned Brezhnev most about the reforms in Czechoslovakia? Why?
   b. Which other reforms might have concerned the leaders in Moscow? Explain your answer. Think about the potential impact on other countries in the Warsaw Pact.

6.1B

The Soviet response

By appointing Dubček as leader in 1968, the Soviets had hoped to calm the growing calls for change. Instead, he began to make reforms, and the Prague Spring represented a huge challenge to Soviet control of Eastern Europe. Leonid Brezhnev, who became Soviet leader in 1964, was faced with a difficult choice. On the one hand, the Warsaw Pact was officially an alliance of independent countries. If Brezhnev chose to interfere in Czechoslovakia, this would show that the Warsaw Pact was not really an alliance but simply a way for the USSR to control the communist countries of Eastern Europe. On the other hand, Dubček's reforms were inspiring people in other parts of Eastern Europe to call for reform in their countries. In Poland, for example, there were several student protests.

The leaders of East Germany and Hungary, along with others, were very concerned about the possibility of unrest in their countries. They looked to Brezhnev to solve the problem. There was a real concern among Eastern European leaders that events in Czechoslovakia could lead to the breakup of the communist bloc.

SOURCE A

A cartoon by the British cartoonist Michael Cummings, published in the Daily Express *newspaper on 24 July 1968. It shows Dubček meeting Brezhnev and other Warsaw Pact leaders.*

"Of course, Mr. Dubcek, we've had to bring a few lady stenographers, one or two secretaries and some tea boys . . ."

The pressure builds: military exercises and the 'Warsaw Letter'

In June 1968, the Czechoslovakian border was chosen as the site for Warsaw Pact military exercises, with Soviet, Polish and East German troops all arriving where their countries bordered Czechoslovakia. This was a clear attempt to intimidate Dubček and show the strength of the Warsaw Pact. The following month, the Warsaw Pact met without Czechoslovakia and issued the 'Warsaw Letter'. The letter said that while each member country was free to make its own decisions, it should not do anything to weaken communism as this risked the whole system across Eastern Europe. Brezhnev met with Dubček but could not convince him to change his approach.

The Soviet invasion

Unable to change Dubček's mind, Brezhnev turned to force. On 20 August 1968, Soviet tanks entered Czechoslovakia and quickly took control of Prague, the capital. There was resistance, but this was dealt with quickly and often brutally. Recognising that the Czechoslovakian forces stood no chance, and to try to save lives, Dubček ordered the army not to fight back. As a final act of defiance, radio stations across the country broadcast reports of the invasion to the outside world. Dubček was arrested and replaced with a new leader in April 1969 who reversed the reforms and was fully loyal to Moscow. The Prague Spring was over.

SOURCE B

A Czechoslovakian woman shouts at Warsaw Pact soldiers in the centre of Prague

Later on…

Czechoslovakia's new leader, Gustáv Husák, reversed all of Dubček's reforms; people who had supported them were removed from their positions in the government. Any opposition or criticism of the government was banned and censorship was extreme. In 1987, when the Soviet leader Mikhail Gorbachev introduced reforms, people noticed how similar they were to Dubček's ideas from 1968. When one of his spokesmen was asked about the difference between Gorbachev's changes and Dubček's, the spokesperson replied, 'Nineteen years.'

Work

1. Why were other Warsaw Pact leaders concerned about events in Czechoslovakia?

2. Look at **Source A**.
   a. What can you see in this source?
   b. What point do you think it is making about the Soviet attempts to peacefully convince Dubček to change his mind about the reforms?

3. Why did Dubček tell the Czechoslovakian army not to resist when the Warsaw Pact troops arrived?

Exam-style question

Write a narrative account analysing the key events of the Prague Spring (1968).

You **may** use the following in your answer:
- Dubček's reforms
- the Warsaw Letter

You **must** also use information of your own. (8 marks)

NAIL IT! For this question, you could write about the causes of the crisis (the reforms), the growing pressure on Dubček to back down, and the Soviet invasion.

Chapter 6: Flashpoint: Czechoslovakia

6.2 How did the world respond to the Prague Spring?

Objectives
- Explore the reactions to the Prague Spring in different parts of the world.
- Assess the impact on superpower relations.

The events of the Prague Spring proved that the USSR would not accept challenges to communism from countries within the Eastern bloc. The clear show of Soviet force in Czechoslovakia did not go unnoticed around the world. What was the reaction within the communist world? How did the West respond? What was the impact on East–West relations?

Inside the Warsaw Pact

While the governments of the other Warsaw Pact countries were fully supportive of the Soviet invasion, many people were less convinced. There were protests in several Eastern European cities under communist control, although these were quickly broken up. There was even a small protest in Red Square in the centre of Moscow, something that had not been seen since the Russian Revolution of 1917. The greatest concern to the Soviet government, however, was the anger felt within the Soviet army. The soldiers had been told that their actions had been requested by the Czechoslovakian people. When they arrived, it quickly became clear that this was not the case. When the soldiers returned to the USSR they told their friends and families what they had seen, and word spread about what had truly taken place.

The emblem of the Warsaw Pact

INTERPRETATION A

Adapted from The 1968 Czechoslovak Crisis: Inside the British Communist Party *by Reuben Falber, published in 1996. Falber was assistant General Secretary of the Communist Party of Great Britain at the time of the Prague Spring.*

What happened that night plunged the world communist movement into crisis. Several communist groups, for the first time in their history, publicly criticised the Soviet Union. Among them were the strongest and most influential parties in the capitalist world. Their relations with the Soviet Party and its supporters became very strained, and in the British Party there opened a wide rift between critics of Soviet policy and its supporters.

Communists in Western countries

Throughout the 1950s and 1960s, there was a small but growing communist movement in many Western European countries, including Britain. For many Western communists, the Soviet invasion of Czechoslovakia was seen as a betrayal of communist values, more about building a Soviet empire than spreading communist ideas. Many were no longer willing to defend the Soviet Union or recognise it as a communist country.

The logo of the Communist Party of Great Britain

Part 2: Cold War crises 1958–70

China

China was the most powerful communist country outside of Eastern Europe, and relations between China and the USSR were severely damaged by the invasion. The Chinese government claimed that the USSR was abandoning communism and that the invasion was just the latest example of this. It is important to remember that China wanted to build its own influence in the world and that an unpopular and less powerful USSR would help it to do this.

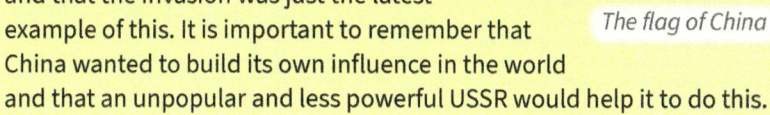

The flag of China

The response from Western countries

The USA quickly criticised the USSR's actions and cancelled an upcoming meeting between President Johnson and Brezhnev. Western European countries were also critical, but no action was taken by the West. The Americans were much more concerned by the events that were taking place in Vietnam and had limited interest in something that had happened behind the Iron Curtain. The USA also did not want to risk a rise in tension, following a period of improved relations since the Cuban Missile Crisis.

The flag of NATO

SOURCE B

Students and the British left-wing political campaigner Tariq Ali (centre) protesting outside the Soviet Embassy against the Soviet invasion of Czechoslovakia, London, 21 August 1968

Meanwhile...

The USA had become involved in the Vietnam War in the 1950s. As part of its policy of containment, America supported the South Vietnamese government against the communists in North Vietnam. By the late 1960s, its involvement had expanded to include hundreds of thousands of American troops. The war was costing huge sums of money and many thousands had died. With no end in sight, the Vietnam War was becoming increasingly unpopular in the USA. The USA withdrew from Vietnam in 1973 and north and south united under communism.

Work

1. Create a spider diagram showing how different countries and groups responded to the Soviet invasion of Czechoslovakia.

2. Look at **Interpretation A**.
   a. According to the interpretation, what was the impact of the Soviet invasion on communists in the UK and around the world?
   b. Why do you think it had this effect?

3. Why do you think Western countries did not intervene in events in Czechoslovakia? Explain your answer.

Exam-style question

Explain **two** consequences of the Prague Spring. (8 marks)

NAIL IT! For this question, you could explain the impact of the Prague Spring on communism in Western countries and the fact that it showed that the USSR was willing to use force to maintain control.

Chapter 6: Flashpoint: Czechoslovakia

6.3 What was the Brezhnev Doctrine?

Objectives
- Outline the key features of the Brezhnev Doctrine.
- Explain the impact of the doctrine on the Warsaw Pact.
- Assess the impact on relations between the superpowers.

After the Prague Spring, the Soviet leader Leonid Brezhnev was determined to avoid a similar situation arising in the future. He gave a speech outlining a policy known as the Brezhnev Doctrine, in which he made clear what was expected of all Warsaw Pact countries. He also made it clear what would happen to those who resisted Moscow's control. What exactly did the Brezhnev Doctrine include? What did it mean for Eastern Europe? What was its impact on superpower relations?

What was the Brezhnev Doctrine?

In November 1968, three months after the invasion of Czechoslovakia, Brezhnev made a speech in which he outlined how he would approach any future challenges to Soviet control of Eastern Europe. He said that he would not allow any communist government to be brought down, either by rebels within the country, or by outside invaders. He made it clear that if any country followed the example of Czechoslovakia, it would face the same consequences. This policy became known as the Brezhnev Doctrine.

SOURCE A
An extract from Brezhnev's speech, 13 November 1968. 'Sovereignty' is the power of a state to govern itself.

> Each Communist Party is responsible not only for its people, but also for all the socialist countries, to the entire communist movement. The sovereignty of each socialist country cannot be opposed to the interests of the world of socialism.

Leonid Brezhnev (1906–82)
- Born in the Ukraine, he served on the Soviet frontline during the Second World War.
- He was supported by Stalin and Khrushchev in his rise through the ranks of the Communist Party. Under Khrushchev, he was one of the most powerful figures in the USSR.
- When Khrushchev was forced from power in October 1964, Brezhnev emerged as his replacement as undisputed leader of the USSR. Unlike on previous occasions, the transition of power involved no violence.

What was the impact of the Brezhnev Doctrine on superpower relations?

Initially, the USA reacted to Brezhnev's speech by calling off all talks between the superpowers. However, this quickly changed as the Americans did not want to undo the progress that had been made since the Cuban Missile Crisis: the two sides had been communicating and working together more effectively on various treaties which aimed to limit the risk of a similar event happening again. The USA therefore chose to see the Brezhnev Doctrine as an internal matter, as it only referred to other communist countries.

The impact on relations between the superpowers was minimal, but the Brezhnev Doctrine did have an impact elsewhere. China saw itself as an equal of the USSR, but many in the Soviet government saw China as more like a satellite state. The Chinese government was therefore very concerned that, if the USSR was unhappy with something that was going on in China, it might invade and begin to control China as it had done with other countries. The principles behind the Brezhnev Doctrine caused grave concern in China and led to even worse relations between the two communist countries. This gave the USA an opportunity to build its own relationship with China.

SOURCE B

A cartoon by John Collins, published in the Canadian newspaper the Montreal Gazette in 1969. The man with the shears in Brezhnev.

Earlier on…

China and the USSR attempted to work together in the interests of communism. In 1950, the two countries signed the Treaty of Friendship. Under the treaty, the USSR provided $300 million in aid to China, although it had to be spent on Soviet products. As long as Stalin was alive, the Chinese communist government of Mao Zedong seemed willing to be guided by its more established ally. However, once Stalin died, Mao wished to be seen as more of an equal, or even as the leader of world communism. The two sides continued to be allies, but the relationship was uneasy.

Meanwhile…

In 1966, 17 years after the Communist Revolution of 1949, China entered a period known as the Cultural Revolution. The Chinese leader, Mao Zedong, aimed to destroy all 'enemies of communism' through a decade of violence and destruction. It is unclear how many Chinese people were killed during this period but estimates range from hundreds of thousands to millions.

Exam-style question

Explain the following:

The importance of the Brezhnev Doctrine for East–West relations.

(8 marks)

NAIL IT! For this question, do not just focus on the obvious point that the Brezhnev Doctrine had a limited immediate impact on relations between the superpowers. You could also consider what poor relations between the USSR and China meant for East–West relations.

Work

1. In your own words, explain what is meant by the Brezhnev Doctrine.

2. Look at **Source A**.
   a. Explain what this source says in your own words.
   b. Why might China see Brezhnev's words as a threat?

3. a. Look at **Source B**. What is happening in the cartoon? Think about what Brezhnev is doing.
   b. What point do you think the cartoon is making about the effect of the Brezhnev Doctrine?

4. Why was the USA willing to accept the Brezhnev Doctrine?

Chapter 6: Flashpoint: Czechoslovakia

Exam practice

How to... answer 'Write a narrative account...' questions

The 'Write a narrative account…' exam question is asking you to write about events in the correct order, with some analysis to show how one event led to the next. 'Narrative' has a similar meaning to 'story', so your answer needs a clear beginning, middle and end. However, it needs to be analytical and not just descriptive.

Here is an example:

> **Exam-style question**
>
> Write a narrative account analysing the key events between 1958 and 1961 that led to the building of the Berlin Wall.
>
> You **may** use the following in your answer:
> - defections
> - the Vienna Summit
>
> You **must** also use information of your own. (8 marks)

Here is one way to answer this type of question.

1 Focus

- Identify what you are being asked to write about in the question.

  In this question, you are being asked to focus on the main events that took place between 1958 and 1961 and led up to the Berlin Wall being built.

- The two bullet points are there to help you find a way into the narrative account, but you don't have to use them. You should try to include at least three events in your answer though: a beginning (an event that started things off), a middle (an event that shows how things developed) and an end (an event that shows how things ended up).

- Identify the event that starts your narrative, the event in the middle and the event that ends your narrative. Think about how each event led to the next one.

  For this question, you could choose the following events:
  - Beginning: By 1958, many people were defecting from East Germany through West Berlin.
  - Middle: Khrushchev issued the Berlin ultimatum in November 1958.
  - End: Defections continued to increase and Khrushchev re-issued his ultimatum at the Vienna Summit. Khrushchev built the Berlin Wall.

2 Add detail

- For each event, make sure you include two or three facts about it. This is where you add names, dates and other details.

72 Part 2: Cold War crises 1958–70

3 Write

- Remember, you are writing about connected events so make sure you write about the events in chronological order and say how one event led to another.
- A 'Write a narrative account…' question must make consistent use of causation language. Use words and phrases like 'Therefore…', 'Subsequently…', 'Consequently…', 'This led to…', 'This resulted in…' and 'Without this…'.
- This exam question is worth 8 marks and you should spend about 10 minutes writing your answer. Top answers will contain a strong paragraph for each event.

Study this sample paragraph. It's the first paragraph of an answer to the question we have been looking at.

> By 1958, the status of West Berlin as a capitalist area within communist-controlled Eastern Europe was causing tension between the superpowers. One of the things that led to the building of the Berlin Wall was the number of defections taking place. The USA had spent money on West Berlin to make capitalism look good, and East Germans could easily see everything on offer because they could still get into West Berlin. This led to many East Germans defecting to live in the West, including highly skilled people. The East German authorities and the Soviets wanted the West to give up Berlin so that defections would no longer be a problem.

- The first sentence introduces the narrative account.
- This second sentence describes the first event in the narrative: defections. This is the first bullet point in the question.
- Detail about the defections is included.
- The last sentence contains analysis, showing how the first event (defections) links to the second event (the Berlin ultimatum).

Work

1. Now have a go at writing the rest of the answer to the question we have been looking at.

2. Then look at the following question and work through the steps above. Which event will you choose to start your narrative? What happens next?

> **Exam-style question**
>
> Write a narrative account analysing Soviet expansion in Eastern Europe between 1945 and 1948.
>
> You **may** include the following:
> - the Yalta Conference
> - Czechoslovakia becoming communist
>
> You **must** also use information of your own. (8 marks)

7.1
The start of détente: hope for better relations

Objectives
- Explain the key reasons for détente.
- Identify the main signs that détente was under way.

Following the Cold War crises of the 1960s, there was a new attempt to reduce tension between the superpowers and limit any further chance of nuclear war. This period of friendlier relations in the 1970s was known as détente. Why was each side interested in détente? What were the signs of détente in action? And what achievements were made in arms reductions and human rights?

Good for everyone? Reasons for détente

By the early 1970s, the Americans and the Soviets both saw the benefits of improving their relationship and reducing the tension of the Cold War. Here's why each side wanted **détente**:

The USSR 	The USA 
• 20% of the USSR's spending went on arms, to catch up with the USA's missile production. This was crippling the economy.  • As a result, living standards for the majority of people behind the Iron Curtain were low. This made communism look bad, and encouraged potential unrest. • The communist bloc would therefore benefit from trading with the West: this needed an improvement in relations.   • Meanwhile, the USSR's relations with China had worsened. This put more pressure on the Soviets to stay relatively friendly with the rest of the world. 	• Living standards remained much higher than those in communist countries, but the US economy was slowing down. The post-war economic boom was over and unemployment had started to rise.  • Consequently, the USA would also benefit from reducing how much it spent on arms. • Until 1973, the USA was still heavily involved in the Vietnam War. This was extremely expensive and had caused division and protests in the USA, as well as international disapproval. Reducing tension with the USSR would help the USA recover from this. 
Both sides	
• By the 1970s, the Cold War had been going on for around 25 years. Politicians at the time accepted that the Cold War was going to be around for a long time. • Both sides were therefore more willing to accept each other's spheres of influence.	

Part 3: The end of the Cold War 1970–91

The Nixon Doctrine

Détente was helped by new leadership in the USA. Richard Nixon had become president in 1969, with Henry Kissinger as his Secretary of State (often considered the USA's chief diplomat). Both wanted better relations with the USSR and China.

The 'Nixon Doctrine' was the term used to sum up the USA's new foreign policy: the USA would remain part of NATO, but would no longer support its allies by sending in troops during conflicts. This was partly in response to the economic cost of the Vietnam War and the political problems it caused at home, but the Nixon Doctrine also reassured Brezhnev that the USA would intervene less in future conflicts.

Limiting nuclear weapons: SALT

SALT stands for Strategic Arms Limitation Talks. Signed in 1972 by the USSR and the USA, the SALT I agreement lasted for five years. The USA and the USSR would restrict their anti-**ballistic missile** sites. These sites contained weapons that could shoot down incoming enemy missiles. They agreed to restrict their submarine-launched ballistic missiles too. However, the agreement did not reduce the number of existing weapons, and both sides still kept their already huge nuclear missile stockpiles.

Other signs of détente

There were many visible signs in the 1970s that tensions were reducing and détente was well under way:
- 1972: Nixon visited Moscow and China.
- 1972: East and West Germany formally recognised each other's borders.
- 1972: the USSR signed a trade deal with the USA to buy American wheat. Later, Soviet oil began to be exported to the West.
- 1974: Brezhnev visited Washington DC, the US capital.
- 1975: US astronauts and Soviet cosmonauts docked their spacecrafts together while in the Earth's orbit.

The Helsinki Accords, 1975

Soviet leaders hoped that détente would mean that the communist system in the USSR and its satellite states would be recognised as acceptable by the rest of the world. Brezhnev also wanted to ensure that the borders of Eastern European countries – changed by the Soviets after the Second World War – were accepted internationally. He was prepared to agree to human rights reforms in exchange.

At Helsinki, Finland, an international agreement on human rights was reached between 35 countries, including the USA and the USSR. The agreement involved:
- a commitment by all 35 countries to improve human rights, allowing freedom of speech, the press, religion and movement
- the West formally recognising the borders of Eastern Europe
- closer cooperation between East and West in terms of their economies, scientific research and culture.

There were reasons to be optimistic about détente. There was a significant reduction in tension, and the threat of a nuclear war seemed to be decreasing. However, mistrust between the superpowers was never far from the surface.

Key words — détente | ballistic missile

SOURCE A
Brezhnev (far left) and Nixon (second right) met several times in the early 1970s, which helped détente to begin

Work

1. Choose three of the signs of détente. Briefly explain why they were important. Be as specific as possible, using all your knowledge of the Cold War up to this point.

2. a. Of all the signs of détente, which ones do you think were most likely to succeed and improve long-term relations?
   b. Which were least likely to succeed?

3. Explain the main difference between the 1947 Truman Doctrine (see pages 24–25) and the 1969 Nixon Doctrine.

Exam-style question

Explain **two** consequences of the decision by the superpowers to improve their relationship through détente.

Chapter 7: Changing relationship between the superpowers

7.2 A false dawn: the reality of détente

Objectives
- Describe the limitations of SALT I and the Helsinki Accords.
- Explain why SALT II was unlikely to succeed.
- Analyse the successes and failures of détente.

Despite the hopes for détente in the early 1970s, there was still a high level of mistrust between the superpowers. There were concerns about the Helsinki Accords being followed by the USSR, and problems were emerging with SALT I. Some people were even worried that the progress made so far was a 'false dawn' – a promising situation that comes to nothing. So were they right? Was it a 'false dawn'? Had détente failed by the end of the 1970s?

Human rights issues

When the Helsinki Accords were signed in 1975, several groups were set up to investigate and monitor how closely countries were sticking to the new human rights agreements. These groups soon found many agreements had been broken, especially in the USSR and the Eastern bloc, where there still wasn't free speech, freedom of movement or freedom of religion for all.

There was clear evidence that **dissidents** – people objecting to the government – in communist countries were being persecuted. For example, in 1977, members of a protest group in Czechoslovakia called Charter 77 were sacked from their jobs and imprisoned, and their children were expelled from school. Jimmy Carter, US President from 1977 to 1981, made his support for dissidents in the USSR clear by talking about continuing human rights problems in his speeches and exchanging letters with some of the dissidents. Soviet leaders were angry about his interference.

The failure of SALT I

Even though SALT I seemed to be a big step towards limiting the spread of nuclear weapons, it was clear that neither side trusted the other and both sides were continuing to develop and position missiles. Weapons technology was also developing rapidly, meaning the specific terms of SALT I were soon out of date.

There were other reasons why further agreements on limiting weapons supplies grew less likely.
- The USSR had been sending large supplies of weapons to Angola and Ethiopia in Africa since the mid-1970s.
- In 1978, President Carter increased the US defence budget – spending more money on weapons again.
- Brezhnev had placed 2000 Soviet troops in Cuba by 1979.
- Members of NATO positioned long-range missiles in Europe in 1979.

SALT II

Even if both sides had stuck to SALT I, its terms were out of date within a few years, so talks for another agreement on limiting weapons began. By 1979, the terms of SALT II had been agreed by the US and the Soviets. This new agreement limited the delivery and placement of nuclear weapons and banned a new, improved version of inter-continental ballistic missiles (ICBMs). It also restricted the use of missile launchers and bomber aircraft.

However, the US Senate (which, along with the House of Representatives, makes laws in the US) refused to officially approve SALT II. The targets seemed too ambitious, and many senators thought the Soviets' actions meant they could not be trusted. Soviets leaders also refused to approve SALT II.

Détente was already in serious trouble by the end of 1979. It was about to be completely wrecked by the Soviet invasion of Afghanistan (see pages 78–81).

Key word — dissident

SOURCE A
This cartoon appeared in an American newspaper in June 1979. It suggests that Carter (left) and Brezhnev (right) committed to the SALT II treaty knowing full well that they each still had huge stocks of nuclear weapons.

SALT II TREATY

Later on…
The failure of nuclear weapons reductions deeply worried many people. In 1981, a group of British women went on a protest march to Greenham Common in Berkshire, England, where 96 nuclear weapons were being stored. It was the biggest female-led protest since the Votes for Women campaign in the early 1900s.

SOURCE B
The women who marched to Greenham Common set up a 'peace camp' there and remained for 19 years. They hoped the British government would remove the missiles and that nuclear disarmament would happen across the world.

Work
1. Make a list of all the reasons why détente could be described as a 'false dawn' – not as successful as it first appeared.
2. Explain in your own words why SALT II failed.
3. **a** Think about how the Soviets would have explained the failure of détente to the rest of the world. Write a paragraph from the Soviet point of view, making sure you highlight all the reasons why the USA could be blamed for relations between the superpowers getting worse again.
   b Now write a paragraph from the American point of view, explaining why the USSR could be blamed for relations between the superpowers getting worse again.

Exam-style question
Write a narrative account analysing the key events of détente in the 1970s.

You **may** use the following in your answer:
- the Helsinki Accords
- SALT II

You **must** also use information of your own. (8 marks)

NAIL IT! We have explored the positive aspects and the negative aspects of détente. Because narrative accounts require you to write in chronological order and link events together, it might be helpful to construct a timeline of all the events of détente – good and bad – before you attempt this question.

Chapter 7: Changing relationship between the superpowers   77

7.3 The Soviet invasion of Afghanistan, 1979

Objectives
- Describe Afghanistan's location in the world and its political problems by 1979.
- Explain why the USSR invaded Afghanistan in December 1979.
- Identify the key features of the Soviet–Afghan War.

In 1979, the USSR invaded Afghanistan. The resulting war between Soviet troops and Afghan fighters was a vicious one, dragging on for nine years and leaving Afghanistan in turmoil. What exactly made Afghanistan so important to the USSR? Why was the Soviet invasion so brutal? And what was the immediate response from the USA?

Why was Afghanistan important to the USSR?

To understand why the USSR was interested in Afghanistan, it is important to realise where it is in the world. For a long time, Afghanistan – though not a wealthy country – was significant because of **geopolitics** (its location and the political importance of this). It lies between Russia and the Middle East, which supplies much of the oil that countries around the world, including the USA and Russia, rely on. The Soviets had some influence over Afghanistan since the late 1940s, but Afghanistan had also been receiving aid from the USA.

Geopolitics became even more important in January 1979 because of events in Iran, a country neighbouring Afghanistan and part of the Middle East, when **fundamentalist** Muslims seized power and put strict Islamic laws in place. The Soviets were concerned about this, because there were around 30 million Muslims in the USSR, many of them living near its borders with Iran and Afghanistan. Soviet leaders were worried that some of these Muslims might try to overthrow communist governments.

Instability in Afghanistan

Afghanistan's government was also very unstable by the end of 1979. In September, an Afghan communist called Hafizullah Amin seized power. Most Afghans were Muslim who hated communism because it rejects all organised religion, including Islam. Amin didn't want to be controlled by Moscow, but his unpopularity amongst Afghan people meant his government was soon completely reliant on Soviet support. A small minority of Muslims declared war on Amin's government and joined a guerrilla fighting force called the **Mujahideen**. Amin therefore relied on Soviet support to stay in power, although the Soviets did not trust him. Brezhnev did not want the situation to get any worse, especially since events in Iran had provided inspiration for Afghan Muslims.

A Afghanistan's location was very important: to the south of the USSR and next to Iran

Key
- The USSR: the republics in the south had significant Muslim populations

Key words: geopolitics | fundamentalist | Mujahideen

Soviet troops invade Afghanistan, December 1979

Brezhnev decided to act. Soviet soldiers invaded Afghanistan on 25 December 1979 and quickly captured Kabul – Afghanistan's capital – and the President's Palace. Within a week, there were 50,000 Soviet troops in Afghanistan and Amin had been killed in the attack. He was replaced by Babrak Karmal, a former leader of Afghanistan who was more pro-Soviet, but who was just as unpopular with most Afghans as Amin had been. Many soldiers from the Afghan army deserted and joined the Mujahideen instead to fight against the Soviet invasion. Around 85,000 Soviet troops were needed just to keep Karmal in power.

Immediate reactions to the Soviet invasion

Brezhnev told the world that the invasion would restore order to an unstable situation, and that Soviet troops would be withdrawn as soon as things calmed down. However, the presence and actions of the Soviet soldiers made this impossible: the Mujahideen were determined to drive them out of Afghanistan and the war would continue until 1989.

US President Carter declared that because the USSR had used unprovoked aggression, the invasion was a threat to world peace. He worried that there could be further Soviet expansion into other parts of Asia. It was clear that the era of détente was well and truly over.

SOURCE B
A Soviet tank in Afghanistan in 1979

Earlier on…
In the nineteenth century, the British and Russian empires both tried to gain influence in Afghanistan because it was crucially positioned between Russia and India, which was then Britain's most important colony. Afghans defeated the British in three separate wars in the 1800s and resisted control by Russia. Afghanistan became known as 'the graveyard of empires'.

Later on…
The Soviet–Afghan War went on for nine years, with the last Soviet troops not withdrawing until 1989. It has been compared to the USA's military involvement in the Vietnam War (1965–75). There were many similarities: both were fighting against guerrilla armies, both used brutal search and destroy methods to find enemy soldiers among civilian populations, both used napalm bombs (which cause terrible fires), both wars dragged on for years costing huge sums of money, and both wars ended in failure for the invading country.

Exam-style question
Write a narrative account analysing the key events that led to the Soviet invasion of Afghanistan (1979).

You **may** use the following in your answer:
- the overthrow of Iran's government
- Amin seizing power in Afghanistan

You **must** also use information of your own. (8 marks)

NAIL IT! Once you have decided which events to write about, you need to make sure you are analysing how one event led to the next. Think about what was motivating each person or group at each stage.

Work
1. Create a spider diagram outlining the reasons why Brezhnev ordered Soviet troops to invade Afghanistan.
2. Explain why you think the Soviets killed Amin, even though he was a communist.
3. Create a 'who's who' profile of the different individuals and groups mentioned in this section.

Chapter 7: Changing relationship between the superpowers

7.4 The USA's response to the Soviet invasion of Afghanistan

Objectives
- Identify the USA's response to the Soviet invasion of Afghanistan.
- Explain how the invasion meant the end of détente.
- Describe the impact on the 1980 Olympic Games.

Many countries around the world were appalled by the USSR's invasion of Afghanistan. It led to the total abandonment of détente and brought back all the tension and suspicion between the superpowers. Why was Carter so determined to react strongly to the invasion? What did the USA do in response? And what was the long term impact on relations between the superpowers?

The Carter Doctrine

US President Carter declared the invasion of Afghanistan a threat to world peace. In January 1980, he announced a series of actions that became known as the Carter Doctrine:

- If necessary, the USA would use its military forces to defend its interests – its political influence and ability to make money by trading – in the areas around Afghanistan and the Middle East. A Rapid Deployment Force was created for this reason, to move troops and equipment quickly.
- A US navy **task force** was sent to the Arabian Sea to protect oil routes to the West.
- The countries bordering Afghanistan could receive military aid from the USA if they asked for it.

Carter hoped that these steps would be enough to encourage Brezhnev to think again about using aggression.

SOURCE A
Adapted from a speech by President Carter to the American people on 21 January 1980

> The 1980s have been born in turmoil, strife, and change. At this moment, massive Soviet troops are attempting to oppress the fiercely independent and deeply religious people of Afghanistan. Since the end of the Second World War, America has led other nations in meeting the challenge of mounting Soviet power.
>
> We superpowers also have the responsibility to exercise restraint in the use of our great military force. The integrity and the independence of weaker nations must not be threatened. They must know that in our presence they are secure.
>
> But now the Soviet Union has taken a radical and an aggressive new step. It is using its great military power against a relatively defenceless nation. The implications of the Soviet invasion of Afghanistan could pose the most serious threat to the peace since the Second World War.

The end of détente

As we have seen, SALT II had still not been officially agreed by either the USA or the USSR. After the invasion of Afghanistan, Carter asked the Senate to delay approving the agreement, and this delay became permanent.

Several trade agreements made during the détente era were also abandoned. For example, a large shipment of grain from the USA to the Soviet Union was cancelled,

Later on...

Both superpowers abandoned Afghanistan after the 1980s. This led to the creation of the Taliban, a fundamentalist Islamic organisation that took over Afghanistan's government.

Osama bin Laden, the al-Qaeda leader who planned a series of terrorist attacks on the USA, including the 9/11 attacks when four planes were highjacked, was a former Mujahideen soldier.

In 2001, in response to the 9/11 attacks, a US-led coalition that included Britain invaded Afghanistan. After 20 years of war, the US withdrew its remaining forces from Afghanistan in 2021, which led to the Taliban seizing control of the country once more.

Key words | task force | boycott

and US companies were banned from selling new technology to the USSR, including oil drilling equipment.

Despite the risk of Soviet retaliation, the USA supported and sent funding to the Mujahideen in Afghanistan, who were fighting a guerrilla war against the invading force. In response, Brezhnev accused the USA of interference, and labelled it as an 'absolutely unreliable partner' for cancelling treaties for no good reason.

The events in Afghanistan were the final 'trigger' that led to the end of détente. It was not long before there was talk of a 'Second Cold War'.

The Cold War hits the Olympic Games

Moscow was due to host the 1980 Olympic Games. In January that year – weeks after Afghanistan was invaded – Carter put pressure on the US Olympic Committee to withdraw its athletes from the Moscow Games. The President remarked that Moscow was now 'an unsuitable site for a festival meant to celebrate peace and goodwill'. A further 61 countries followed the USA's lead and **boycotted** the Games.

In 1984, the Olympics were hosted by Los Angeles in the USA. This time the USSR led a boycott of the Games, followed by 13 other Eastern bloc countries.

SOURCE B
A German photograph of the men's marathon during the Moscow Olympic Games in 1980. The athletes are passing the famous St Basil's Cathedral.

Work

1. **a** Make a list of the different ways the USA responded to the Soviet invasion.
   b Put these in order of how big a threat they were to good relations between the superpowers.

2. **a** Create a spider diagram of all the reasons why détente failed.
   b Discuss with a partner what you think was the most important reason for détente's failure. Remember that just because Afghanistan was the final 'trigger' that led to the collapse of détente, this does not automatically make it the most important reason overall!

Exam-style question

Explain the following:

The importance of the Soviet invasion of Afghanistan in 1979 for the worsening relations between the USA and the USSR. (8 marks)

NAIL IT! When considering the importance of the Soviet invasion of Afghanistan for superpowers relations, remember to include the action of one side and the reaction of the other side.

Chapter 7: Changing relationship between the superpowers   81

7.5
What was the Second Cold War?

Objectives
- Define the 'Second Cold War'.
- Outline Reagan's approach to relations with the Soviet Union.
- Assess the impact of the Second Cold War on superpower relations.

In 1980, Ronald Reagan defeated Jimmy Carter by a huge margin to become US president. In part, Reagan's popularity was due to his criticism of the USSR and his promise to take a tougher stance in the Cold War. After the calm of détente, tensions had started rising again. Some people began to refer to the situation as a 'Second Cold War'. What were Reagan's policies? What was their impact? How did relations between the superpowers change during the 'Second Cold War'?

The election of Ronald Reagan

To many people, détente had seemed to mark the beginning of the end of the Cold War, with the two superpowers working together over matters such as defence. However, events at the end of the 1970s shook that belief. In particular, the war in Afghanistan showed that the USSR was not as committed to the new peaceful and cooperative approach as had been hoped. In the eyes of many US voters, President Carter's determination to maintain a positive relationship with the Soviets made him, and America, look weak. In response, they turned to Ronald Reagan, a former actor who was highly critical of the USSR and promised to be much tougher on it. In the November 1980 election, Reagan defeated Carter by one of the widest margins in the history of US presidential elections. With Reagan's election, it seemed the period of calm may have been over. What became known as the **Second Cold War** was about to begin.

Ronald Reagan (1911–2004)
- Having grown up in Illinois, USA, Reagan became a successful Hollywood actor in the 1940s and 1950s. He worked mostly on low-budget 'B-movies' where the aim was to make lots of films quickly at limited cost.
- In 1941, he became President of the Screen Actors Guild, the trade union for actors. This was during the anti-communist investigations by the US government, and Reagan supported the removal of communists from Hollywood. It was later revealed that he was an informer for the FBI (Federal Bureau of Investigation), telling them about his fellow actors' political activities.
- He was elected governor of California in 1967.
- He was elected US president in 1980 and served until 1989.
- He died in 2004, aged 93. He remains a very popular figure on the right of American politics.

SOURCE A

Ronald Reagan with British Prime Minister Margaret Thatcher at a summit in Italy, 1987. The two had a close relationship and very similar political views.

Key words | Second Cold War | neutron bomb | Strategic Defense Initiative

The 'Evil Empire' and the 'Star Wars' initiative

After he was elected, Reagan convinced the US Congress to increase spending on weapons by 13 per cent. Work began on developing new weapons including the **neutron bomb**, which could kill huge numbers of people by releasing massive amounts of radiation while leaving most buildings and structures intact. The USA also developed stealth bombers, planes that could fly without being detected. In response, the USSR began to spend more and more on weapons, to try to keep up. This restarted the arms race, which had slowed during détente. Reagan did not trust the Soviet leaders and believed that they had used détente to secretly build up their weapons and increase their influence in the world.

In 1983, Reagan made a speech in which he called the USSR an 'evil empire', making a connection to the *Star Wars* films, the third of which had just arrived in cinemas. In *Star Wars*, the heroes, led by Luke Skywalker, battle the evil Galactic Empire. Around the same time, Reagan announced the **Strategic Defense Initiative** (SDI), which became known as the 'Star Wars' programme. This aimed to create a system that could detect and then destroy missiles using laser technology before they could reach the USA. Reagan's aim was to end the MAD (Mutually Assured Destruction) approach that had existed since the 1940s. The SDI was never completed but the ideas behind it caused tensions to rise considerably between the two sides.

Meanwhile…

The reaction to the SDI from around the world, from both allies and enemies, was one of shock. Most saw it as a deliberate and dangerous attempt to provoke the Soviet Union and increase tension. Others questioned whether it was even possible. On 27 March 1983, the *New York Times* described it as 'a projection of fantasy into policy' and said that there was 'no statesmanship in science fiction'.

SOURCE B

A cartoon drawn by Steve Greenberg and published in the American newspaper The Seattle Post-Intelligencer, *in 1987. It shows Ronald Reagan attempting to fly an X-Wing fighter jet from the* Star Wars *films. The speech bubbles also make reference to another science fiction television series:* Star Trek.

Work

1. What made Ronald Reagan popular with many American voters?
2. Study **Source B**.
   a. What is happening in this source?
   b. Do you think the source is supportive of Reagan? Why/Why not?
3. Why do you think Reagan wanted to associate his policies with *Star Wars*?

Exam-style question

Explain **two** consequences of the election of Ronald Reagan. (8 marks)

NAIL IT! Remember, you need to include two distinct consequences in your answer. You could include the Strategic Defense Initiative and increased military spending, and the increased tensions between the superpowers.

Chapter 7: Changing relationship between the superpowers — 83

8.1A Gorbachev's 'new thinking' and the Sinatra Doctrine

Objectives
- Identify key features of Gorbachev's 'new thinking'.
- Describe the summits between Gorbachev and Reagan.
- Assess the impact of Gorbachev's 'new thinking' on superpower relations.

Mikhail Gorbachev, leader of the Soviet Union from 1985, was one of the Cold War's most significant figures. Compared to the Soviet leaders before him, he had a very different approach to solving the USSR's problems. This approach helped to create a big improvement in relations with the USA – and Britain. So, who was Gorbachev? What made his approach so different? And what was the impact on superpower relations?

Gorbachev's new approach

In the years before Gorbachev came to power, there had been a lack of strong leadership in the USSR. Brezhnev died in 1982 after a long illness. The next two leaders, Andropov and Chernenko, were both ill when they took office and died not long after.

In 1985, Gorbachev was chosen as the new leader. At 54 years old, he was the youngest Soviet leader since Stalin. He was clearly different from previous leaders, accepting that the Soviet Union and the Eastern bloc had significant problems. He knew that changes were needed if things were going to improve for the people living there.

Mikhail Gorbachev
- Mikhail Gorbachev (1931–) was born into a farming family and became a lawyer.
- He joined the Communist Party in 1952 and moved into politics.
- By 1980, he was part of the Soviet government. He became leader of the USSR in 1985.
- Although he was able to improve the USSR's relationship with the USA, Gorbachev's attempted reforms of the communist system were less successful.
- After an attempt to overthrow him, Gorbachev resigned in 1991 but remained active in politics.

Urgent problems for Gorbachev

Recent events had put even more pressure on the Soviet system. Under détente, the East had started to trade more with the West, but Eastern bloc countries had also borrowed money from capitalist countries and they were now struggling to pay back these debts.

Most industries in the Soviet Union were also using outdated equipment (such as very old factory machinery) and slow production methods. This made living standards – already poorer in the USSR and the Eastern bloc than in much of the West – even worse. Dissident groups such as Charter 77 in Czechoslovakia were mostly kept under control by the communist authorities, but they still managed to publish leaflets and make radio broadcasts criticising the Soviet system.

Meanwhile...

A nuclear power station in Chernobyl (in modern-day Ukraine) exploded in 1986, leading to the deaths of at least 4000 people, including many who died of radiation poisoning months or years after the disaster. The incident became a symbol of the failures of the Soviet system. The building had been poorly maintained, staff had not been properly trained, and there was a lack of proper safety measures. For weeks afterwards the Soviet authorities tried to cover up the scale of the disaster, rather than admit to the rest of the world what had happened.

SOURCE A
Adapted from Gorbachev's book Memoirs *(1996), written when he was no longer Soviet leader*

The accident at the Chernobyl nuclear power plant was graphic evidence ... of the failure of the old system. I spoke of this at a meeting of Soviet politicians in July 1986. I told them: 'For thirty years you scientists, specialists, and ministers have been telling us everything was safe ... But now we have ended up with a disaster...' Chernobyl shed light on many of the sicknesses of our system as a whole. Everything that had built up over the years came together in this drama: the concealing or hushing up of accidents and other bad news, irresponsibility and carelessness, slipshod work ... This was one more convincing argument in favour of radical reforms.

Part 3: The end of the Cold War 1970–91

'New thinking'

Gorbachev recognised the scale of the Eastern bloc's weaknesses. In industry, agriculture and living standards, the communist countries were very outdated and far behind the West. The Soviet–Afghan War and the new arms race started by President Reagan were costing far more money than the USSR and the Eastern bloc could afford. Gorbachev announced several policies to try to improve the situation, aiming to apply 'new thinking' to the problems of the Cold War. This included:

- **Glasnost:** meaning 'openness'. The aims were to end government corruption, and allow people to openly have new and different ideas from those of the government. Gorbachev hoped it would restore the public's faith in communist leaders, who for many years had punished people who spoke out against communism, and had been ineffective in running their countries.
- **Perestroika:** meaning 'restructuring'. The aims were to change the economy to make it stronger, and allow more involvement by foreigners with different ideas and goods to trade. Under communism, the government set strict targets for industry and was in control of the economy. Now, businesses had more flexibility and could respond to public – not government – demand.

SOURCE B

Gorbachev (left) meeting with British Prime Minister Margaret Thatcher (right) in London in 1984; they met several times during the 1980s. Thatcher worked closely with US President Reagan to build up a better relationship with the USSR. After she first met Gorbachev, she described him as 'a man we [the West] can do business with'.

Work

1. Explain the terms *glasnost* and *perestroika* in your own words.

2. a Create a spider diagram of all the problems the USSR and the Eastern bloc were facing by the time Gorbachev took power in 1985.
   b Which of these problems could have been made better by the USSR improving its relationship with the USA again? Explain your thinking.

8.1B

Gorbachev's impact on superpower relations

Gorbachev did not limit his changing policies and approaches to within the USSR. He also began to make changes outside the USSR, reversing some of the decisions that previous Soviet leaders had made.
- The Brezhnev Doctrine was abandoned. This meant that Soviet control over its satellite states was loosened.
- He planned to end the war with Afghanistan and begin withdrawing troops.

These new measures convinced Reagan that he could work with Gorbachev. As was the case at the start of the détente era, both superpowers saw the benefit of cutting their own spending on armaments (military weapons and equipment).

SOURCE A

Gorbachev wrote about his new approach in his book Perestroika: New Thinking for Our Country and the World, *published in 1987. This is an adapted extract.*

> It is no longer possible to lead countries as if it is still 1947. The main idea of the new political outlook is very simple: nuclear war cannot be a way of achieving any of our goals. There would be neither winners nor losers in a global nuclear conflict. The only way to security is through political decisions and disarmament.

Reagan and Gorbachev met in a series of summits where they held talks on improving relations between the two countries and working to end the arms race. At their first meeting, in Geneva, Switzerland, in 1985, Reagan said to Gorbachev, 'The United States and the Soviet Union are the two greatest countries on Earth, the superpowers. They are the only ones who can start World War III, but also the only two countries that could bring peace to the world.'

\multicolumn{3}{c}{The three main summits between Gorbachev and Reagan}
Date	**Place**	**Main outcomes**
November 1985	Geneva, Switzerland	• Gorbachev and Reagan, meeting without their advisers present, committed to faster action on arms reduction talks and on human rights issues. • Both agreed to reduce their supplies of armaments by 50%.
October 1986	Reykjavik, Iceland	• Gorbachev confirmed that the USSR would begin withdrawing troops from Afghanistan. • Tests on new weapons would be limited by both sides. • Reagan refused to completely give up the SDI ('Star Wars') programme. The summit ended badly as a result.
December 1987	Washington DC, USA	• Both sides promised to get rid of all their medium- and short-range nuclear weapons, including ICBMs. This was written into the Intermediate-Range Nuclear Forces Treaty (INF).

SOURCE B

A photograph of Reagan's wife Nancy (left) and Gorbachev's wife Raisa (right), during the 1985 Geneva Summit. Nancy Reagan was a trusted adviser to her husband, while Raisa Gorbachev was a political science lecturer. The conversations the two women had while their husbands discussed nuclear disarmament were nicknamed the 'tea summits'.

The Sinatra Doctrine

In October 1989, a Soviet Foreign Ministry spokesperson said that the USSR was ready to let the Eastern bloc countries run themselves more independently.

SOURCE C

Gennadi Gerasimov was part of the Soviet Foreign Ministry. This is from a press conference he gave to US reporters on 25 October 1989. In it, he refers to popular American singer Frank Sinatra.

> The Soviet Union recognises the freedom of choice of all countries, specifically the Warsaw Pact states. We now have the Sinatra Doctrine. Sinatra had a song, 'My Way', so now every country decides on its own which road to take. Political structures must be decided by the people and the Soviet Union will accept the rejection of communist parties.

Work

1. In your own words, explain why Reagan was keen to work with Gorbachev on improving superpower relations. Try to write no more than 30 words.

2. Draw a graph to analyse the summits between Reagan and Gorbachev. On the *x* axis, write the years '1985', '1986' and '1987', leaving plenty of space between each one. Write 'Success' at the top of the *y* axis and 'Failure' at the bottom. Then, decide where to place each summit on the graph and write one or two sentences to explain your judgement.

3. a Make a list of Gorbachev's attempts to solve Soviet weaknesses.
   b Make a list of the ways in which relations with the USA improved.
   c Draw a diagram to show how Gorbachev's attempts to solve the weaknesses in the Soviet Union and the improvements in relations with the USA were linked. This could take the form of a flow diagram with arrows.

Exam-style question

Explain **two** consequences of Gorbachev becoming Soviet leader on relations between the superpowers. (8 marks)

NAIL IT! This is a good example of where reading the question carefully will help you write a stronger answer. Here the focus is on superpower relations, so writing at length about policies like *glasnost* will not help you gain high marks.

Chapter 8: The collapse of the Soviet Union

8.2A
How did the Soviet Union lose its grip on Eastern Europe?

Objectives
- Describe the protest movements of the 1980s in the Eastern bloc.
- Examine the impact on the USSR and its control of Eastern Europe.
- Analyse the wider impact on the Cold War.

Gorbachev's new approach – the Sinatra Doctrine – allowed individual governments in Eastern Europe to make their own decisions about the future of their countries. His aim was to strengthen communism by giving people more freedom. In reality, it was clear that by the 1980s many people in communist countries had become fed up with the system and were ready for a much bigger change than Gorbachev had hoped for. How was the Sinatra Doctrine interpreted in Eastern Europe? What was the impact on Soviet control of Eastern Europe? How did this affect the wider Cold War?

New thinking in Eastern Europe

Gorbachev's calls for 'new thinking' were designed to reform and renew communism in the USSR and Eastern Europe. He promised people greater freedom and democracy, and the chance for individual countries within Eastern Europe to make their own decisions without interference from Moscow. This was a major change from the Brezhnev Doctrine, which had stated that if communism was under threat anywhere, the USSR would intervene. From 1988 onwards, people across Eastern Europe began calling for democracy and an end to tight control by Moscow. The maps on pages 88–91 show key flashpoints that took place during this period.

Hungary

In November 1988, the communist leaders in Hungary began introducing reforms. These included allowing trade unions and press freedom. On 24 June 1989, Hungary's first free elections were held and, on 19 August, the government officially opened the border with Austria, allowing people to travel between the countries. On 23 October, exactly 33 years after the Hungarian Uprising began, communist government officially came to an end.

East Germany

On 19 August 1989, a peaceful gathering called the Pan-European Picnic was held at the Hungarian–Austrian border. The idea of the demonstration was to test whether the Soviet Union would try to stop people crossing the newly opened border. When it became clear that it would not, thousands of East Germans escaped through Czechoslovakia and Hungary into West Germany via Austria.

Demonstrations began across East Germany calling for reforms and greater freedom. Erich Honecker, the East German communist leader, hoped for Soviet support, but it did not come. Honecker was removed from power by the communists because he was seen as not handling the crisis well, but the demonstrations continued. Following a major demonstration in Berlin, it was decided that the border with West Berlin should open. On 9 November 1989, thousands of people crossed into West Berlin, some of them taking hammers and axes and smashing the wall as they went. In the weeks that followed, communism collapsed in East Germany, and on 3 October 1990, Germany once again became one country (see pages 92–93).

SOURCE A
People crossing the border into Austria at the Pan-European Picnic in August 1989

88 | Part 3: The end of the Cold War 1970–91

Poland

In 1988, there were strikes across the country, particularly in the shipyards of Gdańsk in northern Poland where workers formed their own trade union called Solidarity. Solidarity quickly grew into a wider political movement, calling for change and for more workers' rights. This was particularly embarrassing for the Polish Communist Party, which was supposed to be the party of working people!

The group's leader, Lech Wałęsa, was invited to meet with the Polish Communist Party. The communists agreed to free elections, with non-communist political parties allowed to stand. These were held in June 1989. Solidarity won every seat in which it was allowed to stand. In the weeks that followed, support for the communists crumbled, and on 24 August, Tadeusz Mazowiecki became the first non-communist prime minister of Poland since the Second World War. Poland became a non-communist country, while still officially remaining in the Warsaw Pact.

SOURCE B

Solidarity protesters in Poland in 1988. The poster translates as: 'Poland – wake up / Poland don't be afraid'.

Key
Eastern bloc members
- Satellite states
- USSR ally until 1948
- USSR ally until 1960

Work

1. **a** What did Gorbachev's 'new thinking' offer Eastern bloc countries?
   b In what ways was this different from the Brezhnev Doctrine?

2. Draw a flow chart to depict events in Poland. It will need three sections: a beginning, a middle and an end.

3. In what ways did the reforms in Hungary lead to changes in East Germany?

Chapter 8: The collapse of the Soviet Union

8.2B

The reforms and revolutions in Eastern Europe were not limited to Poland, Hungary and East Germany. They spread across the Eastern bloc to Czechoslovakia and Romania. These changes had a huge effect on Soviet power, and on the future of the USSR.

Czechoslovakia

Huge demonstrations and strikes in November 1989 led the communist government to realise that it had lost control. Having witnessed events in Poland, Hungary and East Germany, it was now clear that the government would not be able to hold on to power. On 28 November, the communist government announced that it would give up all power and allow free elections. These were held in June 1990. The Velvet Revolution, as it became known (because of the calm and smooth way that it played out), had been almost entirely peaceful.

SOURCE A

Newly elected President Václav Havel addressing huge crowds in Prague on 29 December 1989. Parliamentary elections followed six months later.

Key
Eastern bloc members
- Satellite states
- USSR ally until 1948
- USSR ally until 1960

Romania

Protests began in Romania in 1989. The Romanian government, under the leadership of Nicolae Ceaușescu, was one of the most brutal in dealing with any opposition. At first, the army obeyed government orders to shoot any protesters. This changed on 22 December, when the military forces joined the revolution. As Communist Party headquarters were overrun by rebels, Ceaușescu and his wife escaped by helicopter from the roof but were quickly captured, convicted of various crimes and executed. Free elections were held on 20 May 1990. The Romanian revolution had been much more violent than the others, with over 1000 deaths. Even after the elections, the country faced a number of years of violent unrest.

SOURCE B
Romanian demonstrators watch President Nicolae Ceaușescu and his wife fleeing by helicopter from Communist Party headquarters on 22 December 1989

Meanwhile…
Eastern Europe was not the only place where protesters were challenging the communist authorities. Between April and June 1989, protesters in the Chinese capital, Beijing, demonstrated against the tight controls of the communist government. Unlike in Eastern Europe, however, the Chinese authorities brutally put down the protests and maintained their tight grip on the country.

What was the impact on the USSR and the Cold War?

The Soviet decision not to interfere as communism collapsed in Eastern Europe showed that Gorbachev was serious about giving countries the right to make their own decisions. The speed with which they had abandoned communism, however, undermined the power and control of the USSR, and Gorbachev's ability to govern it. It set off a chain of events that marked the beginning of the end for the Soviet Union itself.

For the USA, the events in Eastern Europe proved its argument that communism only survived because of force and control. However, there was concern that the collapse of the Eastern bloc would leave a power vacuum in Europe. Which governments would be in control? Would there be civil war? Would there be conflict between the newly independent nations, or would they work together and form another powerful bloc? Regardless of these fears, the USSR appeared to be collapsing and the Cold War was coming to an end.

Work
1. a Use the information on pages 88–91 to create an overall timeline of the events that took place in Eastern Europe in 1988–90.
   b Using your timeline, explain how the events could be seen as a chain reaction, with one leading to the next.
2. Why might the decision not to intervene in the revolutions have caused Gorbachev problems in the long term?

Exam-style question
Write a narrative account analysing the key events of the 1988–89 revolutions in Eastern Europe.

You **may** use the following in your answer:
- the Solidarity Movement in Poland
- the overthrow of Nicolae Ceaușescu in Romania

You **must** also use information of your own. (8 marks)

NAIL IT! For this question, you do not need to include everything that you know about the revolutions, you just need to write a clear narrative. For example, you could begin with events in Poland, then show how events in Poland inspired a revolution elsewhere, and finish by saying how the Romanian revolution developed.

8.3 The fall of the Berlin Wall

Objectives
- Describe the events that led to the fall of the Berlin Wall.
- Examine the events of the night it was torn down.
- Explore the consequences for superpower relations.

The opening of the border between Hungary and Austria in August 1989 set in motion a chain of events. These ultimately led, on 9 November, to the fall of the Berlin Wall and the end of almost 30 years of division in the city. How did the fall of the Berlin Wall come about? What happened when it came down? Why was it seen as such an important moment?

The momentum builds

Following the Pan-European Picnic of August 1989, in which thousands of East Germans escaped through the Hungarian–Austrian border with no opposition, there were increasing calls for the borders in Germany itself to be opened. Protests began across East Germany, which the government struggled to contain. On 4 November, a huge protest took place in Alexanderplatz, East Berlin. In response, the new leader of East Germany, Egon Krenz, announced that there would be some limited travel allowed between East and West Germany. However, East Germans would have to apply for permission and, in many cases, they would only be allowed to visit the West for a day, although some longer-term travel would be permitted. At a press conference at 6:00pm on 9 November, a government spokesman, Günter Schabowski, announced these changes to the world's media.

Mixed messages

Just before he spoke, Schabowski was handed a note to say that some permanent **emigration** from East Germany would be allowed. He had not, however, been involved in the decision and did not fully understand the note. When he spoke, he was not clear in what he said. He stated that permanent emigration – moving to live in another country – would be allowed. When he was asked when the changes would come into effect, he said, 'Immediately.' Ignoring attempts by others to correct him, he ended the press conference. Schabowski's words spread quickly, and many East Germans began to gather at the wall. In West Germany, the media jumped on the opportunity and broadcast into East Berlin, encouraging people to head to the border.

SOURCE A
Günter Schabowski speaking at the press conference, 9 November 1989

SOURCE B
East and West Germans gather on top of the Berlin Wall on 9 November 1989. One is using a pickaxe to smash it.

Part 3: The end of the Cold War 1970–91

The wall comes tumbling down

Thousands of East Germans demanded that the border guards let them through. With none of the guards willing to open fire on the crowd, the East German soldiers simply stood back and let the crowd pass. This began at 10:45pm on 9 November at one border crossing point, but quickly spread to others. Those moving from the East were greeted by West Berliners in celebration. Groups of people then began to climb on top of the wall, while others began using whatever tools were available to demolish it. On 3 December 1989, the last communist leader of East Germany, Egon Krenz resigned, along with the rest of the government. On 13 June 1990, what was left of the wall was demolished by the East German army and the country prepared to unite with West Germany in a process called reunification.

Why was this seen as such an important moment?

The fall of the Berlin Wall is seen by many historians as the final major event of the Cold War. The separation between East and West had ended in the city where the tensions had originally begun nearly 50 years earlier. It showed that the USSR had lost control of Eastern Europe and the Warsaw Pact. It was clear that the Soviets were no longer willing, or able, to fight to keep their power and influence. Although the Cold War did not officially end for another two years, 9 November 1989 is often seen as the date at which its end became inevitable.

Key word | emigration

Meanwhile...

One slightly unexpected but famous moment from the time the wall came down was a performance by the American actor and singer David Hasselhoff. Hasselhoff, who is very popular in Germany, performed his song 'Looking for Freedom' from a crane above the wall.

SOURCE C

David Hasselhoff singing to the crowds at the wall on New Year's Eve, 1989

Work

1. Where was the large protest on 4 November 1989?
2. Create a timeline of the events that led to the wall coming down.
3. Why is the fall of the Berlin Wall seen as such an important moment in the Cold War?

Exam-style question

Explain **two** consequences of the fall of the Berlin Wall in 1989. (8 marks)

NAIL IT! Remember to think about consequences in Berlin and Germany, as well as consequences for the wider Cold War.

Chapter 8: The collapse of the Soviet Union

8.4A
The collapse of the Soviet Union and the end of the Cold War

Objectives
- Examine the final months of the USSR's existence.
- Analyse the reasons for its collapse.
- Explore the consequences for the Cold War.

The USSR's loss of control in Eastern Europe showed that it was no longer as powerful as it had once been but the Soviet Union itself remained intact. However, Gorbachev's new approach meant that its future was not secure. Opposition to Gorbachev in his government, together with increasing calls for independence in some parts of the country, meant that the once powerful USSR seemed to be crumbling. How secure was Gorbachev's position as leader? What led to the final collapse of the Soviet Union? What did this mean for its people and the rest of the world?

The end of the Cold War?

One final summit took place between the leaders of the two superpowers. On 2 and 3 December 1989, Gorbachev met with US President George Bush Senior in Malta. Although no official agreements were made, the discussions continued to improve relations and reduce tensions between the two countries. At the meeting, both men spoke of a new, more peaceful era and greater cooperation. Some historians have argued that this summit marked the end of the Cold War, or at least the beginning of the end. There were, however, a few dramatic events still to come!

The Sinatra Doctrine spreads

Beginning with the Solidarity movement in Poland, the end of communist rule across the countries of Eastern Europe was a huge blow to the USSR. Gorbachev had given each of these countries a choice and they had overwhelmingly chosen to abandon communism. The fall of the Berlin Wall in November 1989 showed that Soviet influence in Eastern Europe was at an end. The Warsaw Pact was officially dissolved on 1 July 1991, marking the end of the Eastern bloc.

Although Russia was the biggest and by far the most powerful, it was actually just one of 15 republics that made up the USSR. In 1990, inspired by what had taken place in the Eastern bloc, the non-Russian parts of the Soviet Union, such as the Baltic republics of Estonia, Latvia and Lithuania, began to call for more independence. In March 1990, Lithuania left the USSR. Gorbachev continued to follow his policy of allowing countries to choose for themselves, and it became clear that Estonia and Latvia would not remain part of the USSR for long. Many of those around Gorbachev were very concerned by this development. They thought that losing control of Eastern Europe had been bad enough, but that losing regions of the USSR itself was a step too far. Opposition in the government began to grow.

SOURCE A

Bush Senior and Gorbachev at the Malta Summit in December 1989

Key word: coup

SOURCE B
On 23 August 1989, a huge protest movement took place calling for independence for the three Baltic republics. Around two million people joined hands to form a human chain that ran for 675.5km across Estonia, Latvia and Lithuania.

An attempted coup

Gorbachev had faced enemies within the highest levels of the Communist Party since taking power, but most of them had recognised that the USSR needed to change in order to survive. As problems mounted, opposition to him grew. In August 1991, a group of politicians, leaders of the Soviet army and members of the KGB (the Soviet security agency) attempted to seize control of the country in a **coup**. They held Gorbachev prisoner at his holiday home in Crimea and claimed he was ill. The coup leaders declared a state of emergency and tried to take control of the government.

It was clear, however, that the coup did not have much support. The Baltic states and the mayors of Moscow and St Petersburg refused to support it, and there were protests on the streets of Moscow. Boris Yeltsin, the chairman of the Russian Soviet – the council that governed the Soviet Republic of Russia – called on the people to strike and protest. When soldiers tried to arrest Yeltsin, they were held back by civilians. Standing on a tank and speaking through a megaphone, Yeltsin called the coup a 'new reign of terror'. The soldiers sent to deal with the protests stood down, with some joining the protesters. The coup had failed, and Gorbachev returned to Moscow. However, the coup had shown that Gorbachev's control was weak, and that there were severe political problems within Russia itself. The following month, in September 1991, the independence of the Baltic states (Latvia, Lithuania and Estonia) was officially recognised by the Soviet Union.

SOURCE C
Boris Yeltsin addresses the crowd, and the world's media, standing on a tank outside Parliament in Moscow, 19 August 1991

Meanwhile…
Events elsewhere in the world suggested that the USA was beginning to look beyond the Cold War. In August 1990, Iraq (under the leadership of Saddam Hussein) invaded and took control of the neighbouring country of Kuwait. This gave it control of the country's oil supplies. In January 1991, the USA and a number of its allies led an attack to try to force the Iraqi army out. After five weeks of fighting, the Iraqi army left Kuwait. This became known as the Gulf War, and is seen by many as the first post-Cold War conflict.

Work
1. How many republics made up the USSR?
2. a Write a list of reasons why the coup against Gorbachev failed.
   b What do you think was the most important reason? Explain your answer.

Chapter 8: The collapse of the Soviet Union

8.4B

With Gorbachev's power quickly disappearing and republics leaving the Union, it seemed that the USSR's days were numbered. What were the circumstances of its final collapse? What did all of this mean for the Cold War?

The disintegration of the USSR

On 21 August 1991, Gorbachev resigned as General Secretary of the Communist Party of the Soviet Union and closed down all communist organisations within the government. At the same time, Ukraine announced that it planned to leave the USSR and become independent. Gorbachev attempted to form a non-communist government – the State Council of the Soviet Union – but it had no real power. Between September and October, nine more republics left the Union. On 17 December, Boris Yeltsin, as the first President of Russia, announced that the USSR no longer existed. It could be argued that Gorbachev's reforms achieved some of what he hoped – the people of the USSR and Eastern Europe had more freedom and there was certainly less secrecy – but these things had come about with the total collapse of the system Gorbachev was trying to save.

Boris Yeltsin (1931–2007)

- Born into a poor family, Yeltsin worked his way up through the ranks of the Communist Party, eventually becoming chairman of the Russian Soviet.
- He initially supported Gorbachev's reforms but later said that they needed to go further, calling for full democracy in the Soviet republics.
- Following the coup attempt in August 1991 he became increasingly popular.
- He was elected the first President of Russia in 1991 and served two terms, leaving office in 1999.
- He was a popular figure on the world stage but was also accused of corruption, particularly later in his career. By the time he left office he was extremely unpopular in Russia.

SOURCE A

A cartoon by Etta Hulme, published in the American newspaper the Fort Worth Star Telegram in December 1991. 'Passing the torch' usually refers to someone passing something important, like leadership, onto another person.

GORBACHEV PASSING THE TORCH TO YELTSIN

The end of the Cold War

The end of the USSR left the USA as the world's only superpower. The Cold War was over. Although many in the West saw the collapse of the USSR as a good thing, there was some concern in the US government about what would come next. Whereas before it was concerned only with the actions of one government in Moscow, there were now multiple independent countries, each with their own political ideas. Most concerning of all were the huge stockpiles of nuclear weapons spread across sites all over the former USSR. It was not immediately clear which countries would inherit these, or what their aims would be. There was a very real concern that nuclear weapons could end up in much less predictable hands.

SOURCE B

A cartoon by the American cartoonist Edmund Valtman, published in 1991. The figure is Gorbachev who is watching the symbol of communism – the hammer and sickle – fall apart.

Later on…

Yeltsin was succeeded as president in 1999 by Vladimir Putin. Putin and his supporters have often talked positively about the Soviet era and the strength and power that Russia had at that time. In recent years, as relations between Russia and the West have deteriorated, some commentators have described the situation as a new Cold War.

Work

1. Look at **Source A**.
   a. What is happening in this source? Describe what you can see.
   b. What point do you think the source is making? Think about what Gorbachev is doing to Yeltsin and what this might represent.
2. Why were some in the American government concerned by the Soviet Union's collapse?
3. 'Gorbachev was responsible for the end of the Soviet Union.' How far do you agree? Explain your answer.

Exam-style question

Write a narrative account analysing the key events of the collapse of the USSR.

You **may** use the following in your answer:
- the coup attempt of August 1991
- Boris Yeltsin declaring the end of the USSR in December 1991

You **must** also use information of your own. (8 marks)

NAIL IT! Remember to use causation language to show how one event led to another; for example, how the coup attempt led to Gorbachev losing influence and Yeltsin becoming more powerful.

Chapter 8: The collapse of the Soviet Union 97

8.5 Why did the Cold War end?

Objectives
- Outline the key reasons for the end of the Cold War.
- Explain how each factor played a part.
- Evaluate the factors to decide which was most important.

The rivalry between the superpowers dominated the second half of the twentieth century. The world looked on as the USA and the USSR fought for the upper hand, whether that was in weapons, in the space race or through supporting each other's opponents in proxy wars. Then, after decades of tension, the Cold War ended. What led to the end of the Cold War? What was the most important factor in bringing it to an end?

When did it end?

Historians disagree on exactly when the Cold War ended. For some, once Gorbachev had allowed the Eastern bloc to abandon communism, it was effectively over – particularly when the Berlin Wall fell. For others, it was the meeting between US President Bush Senior and Soviet leader Gorbachev in Malta in December 1989, in which they both promised never to start an actual war – sometimes referred to as a hot war. Others argue that the coup attempt in August 1991 showed that things were still unsettled, and that the Cold War was not finally over until the USSR was officially dissolved in December 1991. Regardless of the exact date, it certainly all happened in a very short space of time. The diagram below summarises the key reasons why the Cold War came to an end.

Reasons why the Cold War came to an end

Mikhail Gorbachev

Gorbachev became leader of the USSR in 1985 and promised to reform it. His two main policies – *glasnost* (openness) and *perestroika* (restructuring) – aimed to save the failing Soviet economy and improve relations with the West. This approach included allowing people to have more of a say in how their countries were run. This policy – the Sinatra Doctrine – led directly to Warsaw Pact members within the Eastern bloc and republics within the USSR abandoning communism and declaring independence. At the same time, Gorbachev aimed to improve relations with the West. He built positive relationships with Western leaders including President Reagan and Prime Minister Thatcher. By weakening the Eastern bloc and ending hostilities with the USA, Gorbachev played a key role in ending the Cold War.

The collapse of the Warsaw Pact

Although the Cold War was a conflict between the USA and the USSR, each country relied on allies to increase their power. When the countries of Eastern Europe abandoned communism and the Warsaw Pact was dissolved (July 1991), the USSR was left on its own, and severely weakened.

Soviet economic weakness

By the 1980s, the Soviet economy was struggling. The government simply could not keep up with American spending on the arms race. Living standards in the USSR were falling, while in the West they were improving for most people. Goods, including new technology, were of a much poorer standard. If things continued as they were, the USSR could be bankrupt, or the leaders could face growing anger from the people.

Part 3: The end of the Cold War 1970–91

Work

1. **a** Which moments do historians argue mark the end of the Cold War?
   b At what point do you think the Cold War ended? Why?

2. **a** Write each of the six reasons why the Cold War came to an end on a separate flashcard.
   b Place them in order of importance, with the most important at the top.
   c Can you make any connections between them? How does one event lead to another? Move the cards around to help you.

Exam-style question

Explain the following:

The importance of Mikhail Gorbachev for the ending of the Cold War. (8 marks)

NAIL IT! Make sure you stay focused on the question. It is asking you about Gorbachev's role in the end of the Cold War, not his role in the collapse of the USSR; these are not the same thing!

The war in Afghanistan

The Soviet invasion of Afghanistan in 1979 was criticised by almost every other country in the world, with the UN calling for the immediate withdrawal of Soviet troops. Even within the Soviet Union there was anger at the war. When Gorbachev came to power in 1985, he withdrew troops from Afghanistan, with the final soldiers leaving in 1989.

The war had cost billions of pounds and the lives of 15,000 troops. The defeat made the USSR look weak, and caused huge problems for the Soviet economy.

SOURCE A
The final Soviet troops leave Afghanistan in October 1989

Ronald Reagan

When he was elected, Reagan was determined to increase pressure on the Soviet government. He increased spending on weapons and the Strategic Defense Initiative (SDI) by huge amounts. This was done to put the USA ahead in the arms race – but also to force the USSR to spend more money on keeping up. He knew full well that the Soviet economy was in a bad state.

Reagan believed that a tougher stance was needed than had been seen under the previous president, and he very openly criticised the USSR. Despite this, he built a strong relationship with Gorbachev, and they were able to work together. Some historians argue that Reagan's approach forced the USSR to compromise.

The attempted August coup and the collapse of the USSR

The attempted coup of August 1991 left Gorbachev in a weak position and the USSR on the verge of collapse. Lithuania had already declared its independence in 1990, and most of the other Soviet republics had done the same by the end of November. Although Gorbachev tried to maintain some control, by the end of the year he was barely able to influence events in Moscow, let alone in the rest of what remained of the USSR. By the time Yeltsin officially declared the USSR's dissolution on 17 December, it was already clear to the world that it was finished. The USA was now the world's only superpower.

Chapter 8: The collapse of the Soviet Union

Exam practice

How to... answer 'Explain two of the following' questions

The 'Explain two of the following' question is asking you to consider the importance of two events, people or developments. What was the significance of the event, person or development for the period of history you are studying?

Here is an example:

> **Exam-style question**
>
> Explain **two** of the following:
> - The importance of the foreign policy of Ronald Reagan for relations between the USA and the USSR. (8 marks)
> - The importance of the Truman Doctrine for relations between East and West. (8 marks)
> - The importance of the Brezhnev Doctrine for Soviet control in Eastern Europe. (8 marks)

Here is one way to answer this type of question.

1 Choose

- The question contains three bullet points and you must choose two to write about. Read all three bullet points carefully before choosing the two you can answer best.

We are going to work through the first bullet point together.

2 Focus

- Identify the event, person or development covered by the bullet point.

    In the bullet point we are looking at, you are being asked to write about Ronald Reagan's foreign policy; for example, referring to the USSR as an 'evil empire' in speeches, and increasing spending on the military and the Strategic Defense Initiative.

- Then identify the importance of the event, person or development to the focus of the question. Think about the importance in the short term and the importance in the long term.

    In the bullet point we are looking at, you are being asked to write about how far Reagan's foreign policy affected the relationship between the USA and the USSR. It is likely that you will argue that it increased tensions in the short term by creating the 'Second Cold War'. In the longer term, you could argue that Reagan's foreign policy resulted in increased military spending in the Soviet Union to keep up with the USA. This led to serious economic problems. You could also look at the rise of Gorbachev and the end of the Cold War and the role that Reagan's foreign policies played in this.

3 Add detail

- Include facts to support the points you are making. This includes dates, as well as the names of people and details about relevant events.

4 Write

- Remember that the question focuses on importance, so use the words 'important' and 'importance' in your answer. You could also use words like 'consequence'.
- Top answers will contain three strong paragraphs: one about the person, event or development, one about the short-term consequences and one about the long-term consequences.
- 'Explain two of the following' questions are worth 16 marks but, in reality, you are answering two 8 mark questions. Spend 10 minutes writing an answer for each bullet you have chosen.

Study this example answer. It is the first two paragraphs of an answer to the bullet point we have been looking at.

> Ronald Reagan's foreign policy had an important impact on relations between the USA and the USSR. During his election campaign and after he was elected President of the USA in 1980, Reagan was very critical of the USSR, saying that previous presidents had been too soft. He called the USSR an 'evil empire' and talked about 'winning' the Cold War. He also massively increased spending on the American military and created the Strategic Defense Initiative, which became known as the 'Star Wars' programme.
>
> In the short term, Reagan's foreign policy had a large impact on relations between the USA and the Soviet Union. After a number of years of improved relations between the two countries, tension between the superpowers increased as a consequence of Reagan's more aggressive policies and language. This started what became known as the Second Cold War.

Notice the use of language that makes it clear that the paragraphs are discussing importance: 'important impact' and 'large impact'.

Both paragraphs begin by setting out exactly what they will discuss. The first paragraph is about Reagan's foreign policy itself, and the second paragraph is about its short-term consequences for relations between the USA and the USSR.

The paragraphs contain lots of accurate detail to support the points being made.

Work

1. Now have a go at writing a third paragraph which explains the longer-term consequences of Reagan's foreign policy for relations between the USA and the USSR. Remember to include specific facts to support your points.
2. Choose a second bullet point from the question and write an answer to it.

Glossary

airlift   using aeroplanes to transport supplies from one place to another

alliance   involves two or more countries agreeing to support each other during a war

allies   countries that agree to work together in international matters and have good relations with each other; by the end of the Second World War, the term 'Allies' (with a capital A) was used to refer to the countries fighting together against Germany, for example, Britain, the USA and the USSR

atomic bomb   a nuclear weapon that was very many times more destructive than any bombs used before

ballistic missile   a flying bomb programmed to hit a particular target; inter-continental ballistic missiles (ICBMs) can travel across whole continents

blockade   similar to a siege; access and supplies to and from an area are stopped, usually to force the people or government being cut off to do something

boycott   to refuse to buy or use something, or to refuse to take part in something

brinkmanship   pushing a negotiation to the edge in the hope of forcing your opponent to back down

capitalism   an economic system under which businesses and individuals are free to make as much money as they can; interference from government is kept to a minimum

censorship   when the press, public speaking and culture are controlled by the government

Checkpoint Charlie   a famous crossing point in the Berlin Wall, heavily guarded and needing permission and paperwork to pass through

CIA   Central Intelligence Agency, the American military organisation responsible for gathering intelligence on other countries

coalition government   a government that is made up of two or more different political parties

Cold War   the term used to describe the tensions between the USA and the USSR between the Second World War and 1991

Comecon   the Soviet recovery plan for Eastern Europe after the Second World War

Cominform   the Communist Information Bureau, designed to bring unity and tighten the USSR's control over East European countries

communism   an economic and political system under which the government controls the economy, and politicians – not businesses – decide what and how many goods are made; in theory, wealth is shared more equally and there isn't a big gap between rich and poor

consumer goods   products that are not absolutely essential, but are commonly used in everyday life, like deodorant or kettles

containment   keeping something harmful under control; the policy of limiting communism to the countries where it had already taken hold

coup a sudden and often violent seizure of power

defect to leave one political system for another, such as leaving the communist East for the capitalist West

democracy this literally means 'power to the people'; a democracy allows its citizens to vote and be represented in government

détente when relations between countries get friendlier; détente is a French word meaning 'release from tension'

dictatorship a type of government that aims to completely control people's lives; people have no say in government under a dictatorship and there is very little freedom

diplomat an official who represents their country abroad, such as an ambassador

dissident someone who challenges or resists a political system

doctrine a belief or set of beliefs held and taught by a group or organisation

dollar imperialism the idea that the USA spreads its power and influence around the world using money

economy the system under which a country's money, trade and production of goods is organised

embargo an official ban on trade with another country

emigration leaving your own country to live in another

ExComm the Executive Committee of the National Security Council; the US committee that advised Kennedy during the Cuban Missile Crisis

exile someone forced to live in a country other than their own, usually for political reasons

free press newspapers, magazines, and radio and television programs are not censored by the government

fundamentalist a religious person who believes that sacred writings should be interpreted literally and that people should strictly follow what they say

geopolitics when the location of countries makes them more or less politically important

guerrilla tactics methods used by people fighting against a stronger army that usually has more soldiers and better weapons; guerrilla tactics often involve hit-and-run attacks, ambushes and blending in with civilians to avoid being attacked

guerrilla war a type of warfare where a smaller, less well-armed group attacks a more powerful enemy using the element of surprise; they often set traps, blow up important buildings, roads or bridges and engage in other acts of sabotage to wear down the enemy

hotline a direct phone line set up for a specific purpose; the nickname given to the direct phone line between the leaders of the USA and the USSR

hydrogen bomb/H-bomb   a more advanced and destructive nuclear weapon; up to 1000 times more powerful than an atomic bomb

Marshall Plan   the recovery programme that provided money and resources to rebuild Europe after the Second World War

Mujahideen   Islamic guerrilla fighters

Mutually Assured Destruction (MAD)   the idea that neither side would use nuclear weapons because to do so would also mean their own destruction

neutron bomb   a powerful nuclear weapon that could wipe out a large population with limited damage to buildings

nuclear weapon   a weapon based on the power created by the splitting of the atom; these weapons cause destruction on a mass scale

propaganda   messages persuading people to think or act in a certain way, usually communicated through posters or radio, but also through artwork, books, television programmes and films; propaganda is generally misleading or untruthful in its approach

proxy war   an indirect war between the superpowers in which one side would provide money or weapons to a group fighting the other; examples include the Korean War, the Vietnam War and the Soviet–Afghan War

purge   the organised imprisonment or execution of a large number of people thought to be disloyal to a government

quarantine   placing someone or something in isolation; during the Cuban Missile Crisis, the USA used this word to describe the blockade it placed around Cuba

reforms   changes made with the aim of improving how a country is run, or the aim of improving the lives of its citizens

reparations   money or goods given to countries that have won a war by those who have lost, to pay for the damage caused

satellite state   a country whose government seems independent, but is dominated by another, stronger country

Second Cold War   the period after 1980 when there was an increase in tensions between the superpowers after the calm of détente

Secretary-General   the senior official in an organisation, such as the United Nations

socialism   a political belief that the community should share available resources equally, often in the form of public ownership of services; in the communist system, socialism is seen as a step on the road to achieving communism

sphere of influence   an area where one country has a huge amount of interest and influence

Strategic Defense Initiative (SDI)
   a planned system announced by Reagan that would allow the USA to detect and shoot down missiles in the air; nicknamed 'Star Wars'

summit   a meeting between world leaders where they talk face to face about key issues

superpower a country that has significantly more power than others, either militarily or economically; it is able to dominate world events

task force a military force used to achieve a specific goal

telegram an electronically delivered message

torpedo an underwater missile

U2 an American spy plane used to gather information on the Soviet Union and its allies

United Nations an international organisation, set up after the Second World War, to resolve conflicts between countries in a peaceful way and deal with major world problems

US Congress the American parliament, made up of the Senate and the House of Representatives

US Secretary of State a senior American politician, often seen as the USA's chief diplomat

Index

9/11 terrorist attacks (2001) 80

A

Afghanistan
   geopolitics 78
   Soviet invasion of/withdrawal from 78–81, 99
   Taliban 80
   US-led invasion of/withdrawal from 80
airlift, Berlin 34–5
alliances
   Grand Alliance 14–15
   Nazi–Soviet alliance 14
allies 8, 14, 15, 16
America *see* United States of America
Amin, Hafizullah 78, 79
anti-ballistic missile sites 75
arms race 36–7, 41, 83, 98, 99
Atlee, Clement 18
atomic bombs 9, 18, 19, 20
   see also nuclear weapons
AVO (Hungarian Secret Police) 42, 43
axis nations 14

B

ballistic missiles 75, 76, 86
Baltic republics 94, 95
Batista, Fulgencio 54
Bay of Pigs invasion 56–7
Berlin
   airlift 34–5
   blockade of 32–4
   division of 30–1, 32
   Khrushchev ultimatum 48
   Wall 50–3, 92–3, 94
Bevin, Ernest 38
'Big Three' 14, 15, 16, 18, 30, 31
bin Laden, Osama 80
Bizonia 32, 33
blockades
   of Cuba 58, 60, 61
   of West Berlin 32–4
Bolsheviks 10
boycott, of Moscow Olympic Games 81
Brazil 63
Brezhnev, Leonid
   Afghanistan, invasion of 79, 81

arms limitation talks 77
Brezhnev Doctrine 70–1
Czechoslovakia, invasion of 67
death of 84
détente 75
and Dubček reforms 65, 66
brinkmanship 59
Britain 36, 77, 79
Bulgaria 22
Bush, George H. W. 94

C

capitalism 10, 12, 31, 65
Carter Doctrine 80
Carter, Jimmy 76, 77, 79, 80, 82
Castro, Fidel 54, 55, 63
   and Bay of Pigs invasion 56, 57
   Cuban Missile Crisis 58, 62
Ceaușescu, Nicolae 91
censorship 12
Charter 77 76, 84
Checkpoint Charlie 52, 53
Chernobyl disaster (1986) 84
China 26, 36, 38, 40
   authoritarian control 91
   Cultural Revolution 71
   and USSR 69, 71
Churchill, Winston
   'Iron Curtain' speech 23
   'percentages agreement' 15
   Potsdam Conference 18
   Yalta Conference 16
CIA 56, 63
coalition government 42
Cold War
   arms race 36–7, 41, 83, 98, 99
   capitalism versus communism 11–12
   Eastern bloc 23, 66, 68, 89, 91, 94, 98
   end of 93, 94–9
   Second Cold War 82–3
   start of 20
   superpower rivalry 8–9
Comecon 28–9, 43
Cominform 25, 28, 29
communism
   capitalism comparison 11
   collapse of in Eastern Europe 88–91
   containment of 24
   in Cuba 54–5

'domino theory' 24, 56
Gorbachev's 'new thinking' 85
Kennedy's West Berlin speech 53
origin of 10
in South America 29, 63
threat of 12, 41
in USA 82
in Western Europe 27, 68
world communism leadership 71
consumer goods 33
containment policy 24, 69
coup, against Gorbachev 95, 99
Cuba
   Bay of Pigs invasion 56–7
   blockade of 58, 60, 61
   removal of Soviet missiles from 61, 62
   revolution 54–5
   Soviet missiles in 58
   and superpowers 55
   support of communist fighters 63
Cuban Missile Crisis 58–63
   blockade of Cuba 58, 60, 61
   nuclear war, danger of 60, 61
   removal of Soviet missiles from Cuba 61, 62
   Soviet missiles in Cuba 58
   Soviet submarine, depth-charging of 60
   timeline 59, 61
   U2 spy plane, shooting down of 60
Cultural Revolution 71
Czechoslovakia
   communist takeover of 22
   dissidents 76, 84
   end of communist rule 90
   Prague Spring 64–9
   Soviet invasion of 67

D

de Gaulle, Charles 30
decolonisation 8
DEFCON system 58, 59
defections 48, 50
democracy 10, 11, 12, 24, 31
Democratic Republic of Germany (GDR)
   see East Germany
destalinisation 40–1
détente 74–7

arms limitation talks   75, 76, 80
   benefits of for superpowers   74
   end of   79, 80–1
Deutsche Mark   32
dictatorship   10, 11, 12, 13, 17, 24, 31, 43, 55
diplomats   21
dissidents   76, 84
doctrines   24
'dollar imperialism'   28
'domino theory'   24, 56
Dubček, Alexander
   reforms of   64–5, 67
   and Soviet invasion of Czechoslovakia   67

E
East Berlin   50–3, 92–3, 94
East Germany
   blockade of Berlin   33
   communist takeover of   22
   currency   32
   and division of Germany   35
   economy   31
   emigration   92
   end of communist rule   88, 93
   fall of Berlin Wall   92–3, 94
   refugee crisis   48, 50
   revolt against communist rule   41
Eastern bloc   66, 68, 89, 98
   collapse of   91, 94
Eastern Europe
   collapse of communist rule   88–91
   Cominform   25
   'new thinking' in   88–91
   Potsdam Conference   19
   satellite states   22, 41, 89
   Soviet occupation of   18
   Soviet 'spheres of influence'   16, 17
   see also Bulgaria; Czechoslovakia; East Germany; Hungary; Poland; Romania; Ukraine; Yugoslavia
economies
   capitalism versus communism   11
   East Germany   31
   USA   8, 12, 74
   USSR   12, 74, 84, 98
Egypt   45
Eisenhower, Dwight D.
   'domino theory'   24
   Khrushchev meeting   40

   and Suez Crisis   45
   and U2 spy planes   48
embargoes   55
emigration   92
Estonia   94, 95
'evil empire', portrayal of USSR as   83
exam practice   46–7, 72–3, 100–1
ExComm   58
exiles, Cuban   56, 57

F
Fechter, Peter   53
Federal Republic of Germany (FRG) see West Germany
France   30, 36
fundamentalists   78, 80

G
GDR (Democratic Republic of Germany) see East Germany
Geneva Summit (1985)   86, 87
geopolitics   78
Germany
   division of   17, 19, 30–1, 32, 35
   Second World War   14, 16
   see also East Germany; West Germany
glasnost (openness)   85
Gorbachev, Mikhail   67, 84–91, 94–7, 98
   and Afghanistan war   99
   collapse of USSR   97
   coup attempt against   95, 99
   and pressures on Soviet system   84
   Reagan meetings   86, 99
   resignation of   96
   and superpower relations   86
Gorbachev, Raisa   87
Grand Alliance   14–15
Greece   24, 27
Greenham Common protests   77
Guatemala   29
guerrilla tactics   45
guerrilla wars   54, 63, 78, 81
Guevara, Ernesto 'Che'   54, 55
Guinea   56
Gulf War   95

H
H-bombs (hydrogen bombs)   36, 37
Havel, Václav   90
Helsinki Accords   75, 76

'hibakusha' (person affected by radiation exposure)   20
Hiroshima, atomic bombing of   20
Hitler, Adolf   18
Honecker, Erich   88
'hotline'   63
human rights   75, 76
Hungary
   communist takeover of   22
   end of communist rule   88
   Uprising   42–5
hydrogen bombs (H-bombs)   36, 37

I
India   36
inter-continental ballistic missiles (ICBMs)   76, 86
Iraq   95
'Iron Curtain'   22–3, 39
Israel   36

J
Japan
   atomic bombing of   19, 20
   Pearl Harbor attack   14
   US planned invasion of   16

K
Kádár, János   45
Karmal, Babrak   79
Kennan, George   21
Kennedy, John Fitzgerald
   Bay of Pigs invasion   56–7
   and Berlin Wall   52
   Cuban Missile Crisis   58, 61, 62
   Vienna Summit   49
   West Berlin speech   53
KGB (secret police)   12, 40
Khrushchev, Nikita
   Berlin ultimatum   48
   Berlin Wall   50, 53
   Cuban Missile Crisis   59, 60, 61, 62
   and Eastern bloc   41
   Eisenhower meeting   40
   Hungarian Uprising   42, 44
   Vienna Summit   49
Korean War   40
Krenz, Egon   92, 93
Kuwait   95

L

Latin America   29, 63
Latvia   94, 95
Lenin, Vladimir   10
Lithuania   94, 95
Long Telegram (Kennan)   21

M

McCarthy, Joseph   41
MAD *see* Mutually Assured Destruction
Malta Summit (1989)   94, 98
Mao Zedong   38, 71
Marshall, George   26
Marshall Plan/Aid   26–9, 31
Mazowiecki, Tadeusz   89
Moscow Conference (1944)   15
Moscow Olympic Games, boycott of   81
Mujahideen   78, 79, 81
Mutually Assured Destruction (MAD)   9, 36, 83

N

Nagasaki, atomic bombing of   20
Nagy, Imre   43, 45
Nasser, Abdul   45
NATO (North Atlantic Treaty Organization)   38–9
Nazi–Soviet alliance   14
neutron bombs   83
Nixon Doctrine   75
North Atlantic Treaty Organization (NATO)   38–9
North Korea   36, 40
North Vietnam   63, 69
Novikov Telegram   21
Novotný, Antonín   64
Nuclear Non-proliferation Treaty   63
nuclear powers   36
nuclear war   60, 61
nuclear weapons   9, 18, 19, 36, 37, 41, 83
  arms reduction talks   75, 76, 80, 86
  and collapse of USSR   97
  in Cuba   58
  Greenham Common protests   77
  Limited Test Ban Treaty   63
  use against Japan   20

O

Olympic Games, boycott of   81

P

Pakistan   36
Pan-European Picnic   88, 92
Paris Summit (1960)   48
Pearl Harbor attack   14
'percentages agreement'   15
perestroika (restructuring)   85
Point Four Program   27
Poland
  communist takeover of   18, 22
  end of communist rule   89
  reforms   42
  revolt against communist rule   41
  and Yalta Conference   17
Potsdam Conference (1945)   18–19, 30
Prague Spring   64–9
propaganda   9, 12, 53
proxy wars   9
purges   43
Putin, Vladimir   97

Q

quarantine   58, 60

R

radiation sickness   20
Rákosi, Mátyás   22, 42, 43
Reagan, Nancy   87
Reagan, Ronald
  election of   82
  Gorbachev meetings   86
  'Star Wars' initiative   83
  Thatcher meetings   82
Red Army   18, 41
  see also Soviet army
'Red Scare'   41
reforms
  Czechoslovakia   64–5, 67
  Eastern Europe   88–91
  Hungary   43
  Poland   42
  USSR   85
refugees   48, 50
reparations   16, 17, 31
Reykjavik Summit (1986)   86
Romania   22, 91
Roosevelt, Franklin D.   15, 16, 18
Russia   10, 13, 79, 94
  see also Union of Soviet Socialist Republics

S

SALT (Strategic Arms Limitation Talks)   75, 76, 80
satellite states   22, 41, 89
Schabowski, Günter   92
SDI *see* Strategic Defense Initiative
Second Cold War   82–3
Second World War
  allies   8, 13, 14–15
  atomic bombing of Japan   19, 20
  axis nations   14
  economic effects of   26
  Grand Alliance   14–15
  Moscow Conference   15
  Potsdam Conference   18–19, 30
  Soviet advance into Eastern Europe   18
  Yalta Conference   16–17, 30, 52
secret police
  East German   31
  Hungarian   42, 43
  Soviet   12, 23, 40
Secretary-General, United Nations   59
Sinatra Doctrine   87, 88, 94, 98
Sino–Soviet relations   69, 71
socialism   64
Solidarity   89
South America   29, 63
South Korea   40
South Vietnam   63, 69
Soviet army   68
  see also Red Army
Soviet Union *see* Union of Soviet Socialist Republics
space race   37
'spheres of influence'   8, 16, 17
spy planes   48, 49, 58, 60
Stalin, Joseph   12, 13, 14, 31
  and atomic bomb   20, 21
  Berlin blockade   32–4, 35
  Comecon   28
  Cominform   25
  death of   40
  Eastern Europe   22
  and Marshall Plan   28
  Moscow Conference   15
  and NATO formation   38
  'percentages agreement'   15
  Potsdam Conference   19
  Yalta Conference   16
'Star Wars' initiative   83
Stasi (secret police)   31

Strategic Arms Limitation Talks (SALT)   75, 76, 80
Strategic Defense Initiative (SDI)   83, 86
Suez Crisis   45
summits   48–9, 86, 87, 94, 98
superpowers   8, 9, 80
   and Brezhnev Doctrine   71
   Cuba and   55
   détente, benefits of   74
   Gorbachev's impact on superpower relations   86
   summits   48–9, 86, 87, 94, 98

T

Taliban   80
task forces   80
Tehran Conference (1943)   15
telegrams   21
Thatcher, Margaret   82, 85
'the thaw'   40–1
timelines   6–7, 59, 61
Tito, General   29
torpedoes   60
Truman, Harry S.
   atomic bombing of Japan   20
   election of   24, 25
   Potsdam Conference   18, 19
   Truman Doctrine   24–5
'Trummelfrauen' (rubble women)   30
Turkey, removal of US missiles from   61, 62

U

U2 spy planes   48, 49, 58, 60
Ukraine   96
Ulbricht, Walter   50, 51
Union of Soviet Socialist Republics (USSR)
   Afghanistan, invasion of/withdrawal from   78–81, 99
   arms limitation talks   75, 76, 80
   arms race   36–7, 41, 83, 98, 99
   Baltic republics   94, 95
   Berlin blockade   32–4
   Brezhnev Doctrine   70–1
   Chernobyl disaster   84
   and China   69, 71
   collapse of   94–7
   communist criticism of   68
   communist system   11
   coup attempt against Gorbachev   95, 99
   Cuba, support for   55
   Cuban Missile Crisis   58–63
   Czechoslovakia, invasion of   67
   destalinisation   40–1
   détente   74–7
   dictatorship   11, 12, 13
   dissidents   76
   distrust of USA   9, 20, 21, 29
   and Dubček reforms   65, 66
   economy   12, 74, 84, 98
   'evil empire' portrayal   83
   German invasion of   14
   Gorbachev's 'new thinking'   67, 84–91, 94–7
   Grand Alliance   14–15
   and Hungarian Uprising   42, 44
   Moscow Conference   15
   Potsdam Conference   18–19, 30
   and Prague Spring   65, 66
   republics of   9, 94, 96
   SALT I and II   75, 76, 80
   satellite states   22, 89
   Second World War   8, 14–15
   secret police   12, 23, 40
   Sinatra Doctrine   87, 88, 94, 98
   Sino-Soviet relations   69, 71
   space race   37
   'sphere of influence'   8, 16, 17
   'the thaw'   40–1
   US–Soviet relations   9, 20, 21, 29, 40–1
   Yalta Conference   16–17, 30, 52
   see also Russia
United Nations (UN)   15, 59
United States of America (USA)
   arms limitation talks   75, 76, 80
   arms race   36–7, 41, 83, 98, 99
   Bay of Pigs invasion   56–7
   and Berlin Wall   52–3
   and Brezhnev Doctrine   71
   capitalist system   11, 12
   and collapse of Eastern bloc   91
   and collapse of USSR   97
   communist threat   12, 24, 41
   communists in   82
   containment policy   24, 69
   Cuban Missile Crisis   58–63
   democracy   10, 11, 12
   détente   74–7
   distrust of USSR   9, 13, 21, 29
   economy   8, 12, 74
   Marshall Plan/Aid   26–9
   Potsdam Conference   18–19, 30
   proxy wars   9
   'Red Scare'   41
   SALT I and II   75, 76, 80
   Second World War   8, 14–15
   and Soviet invasion of Afghanistan   80–1
   and Soviet invasion of Czechoslovakia   69
   space race   37
   'sphere of influence'   8
   'the thaw'   40–1
   US–Soviet relations   9, 13, 21, 29, 40–1
   Yalta Conference   16–17, 30, 52
US Congress   24
US Secretary of State   26
USA see United States of America
USSR see Union of Soviet Socialist Republics

V

Velvet Revolution   90
Vienna Summit (1961)   49
Vietnam   63
Vietnam War   69

W

Wałęsa, Lech   89
'Warsaw Letter'   66
Warsaw Pact   38–9, 66, 68, 94, 98
Washington Summit (1987)   86
West Berlin
   blockade of   32–4
   Kennedy's visit to   53
   rebuilding of   31
   Wall   50–3, 88, 92–3, 94
West Germany   31, 35, 38, 48
   fall of Berlin Wall   92–3, 94
Western Europe
   communists in   11, 27, 68
   Marshall Plan/Aid   26, 27

Y

Yalta Conference (1945)   16–17, 30, 52
Yeltsin, Boris   95, 96, 99
Yugoslavia   29

Acknowledgements

The publishers would like to thank the following for permission to use copyright material:

Excerpt from **W. Ulbricht:** letter to Khrushchev on Closing the Border Around West Berlin, 15 September 1961, found at The Wilson Center Digital Archive, Published in CWIHP Working Paper No. 5, "Ulbricht and the Concrete 'Rose.'" Translated for CWIHP by Hope Harrison. SED Archives, IfGA, ZPA, Central Committee files, Walter Ulbricht's office, Internal Party Archive, J IV 2/202/130. http://digitalarchive.wilsoncenter.org/document/116212 English Translation reproduced with permission from The Cold War International History Project.

Excerpt from **B. Russell and A. Einstein**, Russell-Einstein Manifesto, 9 July 1955. Adapted with permission from Pugwash Conferences on Science & World Affairs.

W. S. Churchill: *An Iron Curtain has Descended*, speech made at Fulton, Missouri, 5 March 1946. (W. S. Churchill, 1946). Reproduced with permission of Curtis Brown, London on behalf of The Estate of Winston S. Churchill © The Estate of Winston S. Churchill.

R. Falber: *The 1968 Czechoslovak Crisis: Inside the British Communist Party* (Socialist History Society, 1996). Adapted with permission from The Socialist History Society.

R. G. Suny: *The Soviet Experiment: Russia, the USSR, and the successor states* (Oxford University Press, 1998). Reproduced with permission of Oxford University Press through PLSclear.

Cover: Everett Collection Inc / Alamy Stock Photo. **Photos: p6(c):** Hulton Archive / Getty Images; **p6(bl):** David Lichtneker / Alamy Stock Photo; **p6(br):** Keystone-France / Getty Images; **p7(t):** Sueddeutsche Zeitung Photo / Alamy Stock Photo; **p7(bl):** Getty Images / Handout / Getty Images; **p7(br):** peter jordan / Alamy Stock Photo; **p9:** Album / Alamy Stock Photo; **p10:** Pictures Now / Alamy Stock Photo; **p12(t):** World History Archive / Alamy Stock Photo; **p12(b):** Tobie Mathew / Bridgeman Images; **p15(l):** Bettmann / Getty Images; **p15(c):** ZUMA Press, Inc. / Alamy Stock Photo; **p15(r):** David Cole / Alamy Stock Photo; **p16:** Niday Picture Library / Alamy Stock Photo; **p17:** Pictorial Press Ltd / Alamy Stock Photo; **p18:** Everett Collection Historical / Alamy Stock Photo; **p19:** Paul Carmack / The Christian Science Monitor; **p20:** Hulton Archive / Getty Images; **p21:** David Low / London Evening Standard; **p25(t):** Everett Collection Inc / Alamy Stock Photo; **p25(b):** Punch Limited; **p27(r):** Granger Historical Picture Archive / Alamy Stock Photo; **p27(l):** Everett Collection Historical / Alamy Stock Photo; **p28:** SPUTNIK / Alamy Stock Photo; **p29:** Archives Charmet / Bridgeman Images; **p30:** dpa picture alliance / Alamy Stock Photo; **p31:** Everett Collection Historical / Alamy Stock Photo; **p32:** Keystone Press / Alamy Stock Photo; **p35(t):** David Lichtneker / Alamy Stock Photo; **p35(b):** Punch Limited; **p36:** GraphicaArtis / Getty Images; **p37:** Pictorial Press Ltd / Alamy Stock Photo; **p38:** Solo Syndication; **p40:** Everett Collection Historical / Alamy Stock Photo; **p41:** Keystone Press / Alamy Stock Photo; **p42:** Keystone / Staff / Getty Images; **p43:** Keystone Press / Alamy Stock Photo; **p44:** AFP / Getty Images; **p46:** Monkey Business Images / Shutterstock; **p49(l):** SPUTNIK / Alamy Stock Photo; **p49(r):** British Cartoon Archive / New Statesman; **p51:** dpa picture alliance / Alamy Stock Photo; **p52:** Universal Art Archive / Alamy Stock Photo; **p54:** Michael Honegger / Alamy Stock Photo; **p55(r):** TNT Magazine Pixate Ltd / Alamy Stock Photo; **p55(l):** nik wheeler / Alamy Stock Photo; **p57:** MIGUEL VINAS / Getty Images; **p58:** Hulton

Archive / Getty Images; **p60:** Keystone-France / Getty Images; **p61:** Solo Syndication; **p62(tl):** World History Archive / Alamy Stock Photo; **p62(b):** Science History Images / Alamy Stock Photo; **p62(tr):** John Frost Newspapers / Alamy Stock Photo; **p63:** vint3 / Alamy Stock Photo; **p65:** CTK / Alamy Stock Photo; **p66:** Express Syndication Ltd/ topfoto; **p67:** Bettmann / Getty Images; **p69:** Ballard / Getty Images; **p70:** Keystone Press / Alamy Stock Photo; **p71:** McCord Museum; **p72:** Monkey Business Images/ Shutterstock; **p75:** mccool / Alamy Stock Photo; **p77(t):** Reprinted with permission from Baaske Cartoon; **p77(b):** Mike Goldwater / Alamy Stock Photo; **p79:** Getty Images / Handout / Getty Images; **p81:** Bundesarchiv; **p82:** peter jordan / Alamy Stock Photo; **p83:** Tribune Publishing Company; **p84:** Everett Collection Inc / Alamy Stock Photo; **p85:** peter jordan / Alamy Stock Photo; **p87:** Dieter Endlicher / AP / Shutterstock; **p88:** Votava/AP/Shutterstock; **p89:** agencja FORUM / Alamy Stock Photo; **p90:** CTK / Alamy Stock Photo; **p91:** REUTERS / Alamy Stock Photo; **p92(l):** dpa picture alliance / Alamy Stock Photo; **p92(r):** Sueddeutsche Zeitung Photo / Alamy Stock Photo; **p93:** dpa picture alliance / Alamy Stock Photo; **p94:** JONATHAN UTZ / Getty Images; **p95(t):** Tiit Veermae / Alamy Stock Photo; **p95(b):** Wojtek Laski / Getty Images; **p96(t):** Photo 12 / Alamy Stock Photo; **p96(b):** University of Texas at Arlington Libraries, Special Collections (CC BY-NC 4.0); **p97:** Library of Congress Prints and Photographs Division Washington, D.C. 20540 USA; **p98:** JONATHAN UTZ / Getty Images; **p99(bl):** SPUTNIK / Alamy Stock Photo; **p99(bc):** World History Archive / Alamy Stock Photo; **p99(br):** Wojtek Laski / Getty Images.

Artwork by Aptara, Kamae Design, Moreno Chiacchiera, and Q2A Media.

Although we have made every effort to trace and contact all copyright holders before publication this has not been possible in all cases. If notified, the publisher will rectify any errors or omissions at the earliest opportunity.

Links to third party websites are provided by Oxford in good faith and for information only. Oxford disclaims any responsibility for the materials contained in any third party website referenced in this work.